GET THE SALT OUT

Other Books in This Series by Ann Louise Gittleman

GET THE
SALT OUT

**501 Simple Ways to Cut the Salt
Out of Any Diet**

Ann Louise Gittleman, M.S., C.N.S.

THREE RIVERS PRESS
NEW YORK

To James . . . just because

Permission to reprint already published recipes
appear on pages 229–233.

Published by Three Rivers Press, New York, New York.
Member of the Crown Publishing Group.

Random House, Inc. New York, Toronto, London, Sydney, Auckland
www.randomhouse.com

THREE RIVERS PRESS is a registered trademark and the Three Rivers Press
colophon is a trademark of Random House, Inc.

Printed in the United States of America

Design by M. Kristen Bearse

Library of Congress Cataloging-in-Publication Data
Gittleman, Ann Louise.
Get the salt out : 501 simple ways to cut the salt out of any diet /
by Ann Louise Gittleman.
Includes bibliographical references and index.
1. Salt-free diet. I. Title.
RM237.8.G58   1997   613.2'85—dc21   96-49042

ISBN 0-517-88654-5

10 9

CONTENTS

ACKNOWLEDGMENTS

My sincere thanks to Leslie Meredith of Crown Publishers, who commissioned me to do this project in the first place. Also many thanks to Karin Wood and Andrew Stuart, who were extremely helpful in editing and finetuning the manuscript. Thanks to Elizabeth Keeler Love, whose dedicated office assistance made my job that much easier. Many thanks also to Helen Smith for her continual support and to Holly Sollars, whose culinary expertise helped this book immensely. And last but not least, my most grateful appreciation to Melissa Diane Smith, whose talent, devotion, and creativity allowed this book to materialize in its present form.

The Facts about
Salt and Sodium

A ll of us should restrict our intake of common table salt.
This is one recommendation on which health experts agree.
Every major medical and nutritional organization—from
the American Heart Association to the American Medical
Association to the United States Department of Agriculture—
says the same thing: salt, in the amount we currently consume,
seriously jeopardizes our health.

Just how much salt do we consume? According to *The
Sodium Counter* (Pocket Books, 1993), the average American's
salt intake is two to three teaspoons a day. This may not sound
like a lot, but it provides 4,000 to 6,000 milligrams of sodium a
day—which can be double the Food and Drug Administration's
maximum recommended daily quantity of 2,400 milligrams.

No other mammal eats this much salt, and no other mammal has the health problems we do. High blood pressure, for
example, was never even seen in animals until researchers found
they could induce it either by surgery or by introducing large
amounts of salt into animals' diets.

If salt added to your food seems like a natural and necessary part of life to you, consider that the human race is about
fifty thousand years old and we discovered salt only about six

thousand years ago. (Sanskrit, one of the oldest human languages, does not even have a word for salt.) Throughout history, most human cultures have not used salt; the sodium that occurred naturally in their diets provided all they required.

In *The Paleolithic Prescription* (Harper & Row, 1988), anthropological researchers S. Boyd Eaton, M.D., Marjorie Shostak, and Melvin Konner, Ph.D., point out that our hunter-gatherer ancestors consumed approximately 700 milligrams of sodium a day—the equivalent found in one-third of a teaspoon of salt. While the amount of stress that we experience in our modern-day lives may require us to consume slightly more sodium than our ancestors did, it is clear that today we consume far more than we need.

We unknowingly absorb excessive salt not only from food, but also from an unsuspected source: the salt-softened water in which we bathe. Since the American Heart Association now warns that salt-softened water can cause an elevated sodium level, many health-conscious Americans no longer drink salt-softened water. Few of us, however, realize that we receive a lot of unwanted sodium every time we take a shower or a bath or wash clothes in softened water. Sodium is very efficiently absorbed through the skin, and topically ingested salt has become a common culprit of excess sodium.

The sodium we consume from food and water is only part of the problem. The highly refined nature of common table salt is the other part. Although our bodies are not designed to handle large amounts of sodium, healthy individuals usually can tolerate some excess sodium if it is in a naturally occurring form that our bodies can readily use or excrete. Commercial table salt used in our food and to soften water, however, is the furthest thing from this ideal. During the refining of table salt, natural sea salt or rock salt is stripped of more than sixty trace minerals

and essential macro-nutrients, leaving a single chemical compound: sodium chloride. This minerally unbalanced salt is then
treated with chemicals such as bleaches, conditioners, and anticaking agents, rendering a difficult-to-absorb salt that stresses
our systems and invariably causes severe health problems.

Most of us already know that excessive salt consumption
contributes to the development of high blood pressure, but
recent research shows that it is also associated with strokes,
migraine headaches, and osteoporosis among other health problems. (For a complete listing of the ailments associated with salt
consumption, see the section The Problems with Salt and
Sodium in this Preface.)

Some of you might be well aware of the hazards of refined
salt and are eager to move on to the tips for reducing your
intake. If you are, please understand this: like fat, sodium is
misunderstood by the public. Sodium and fat are nutrients we
need for health, but not all forms of them are healthy. *Refined or
common table salt is an unhealthy form of sodium we all should
avoid.*

If you would like to understand better the vital distinction
between sodium and refined salt, keep reading. If, however, you
decide to skip the next section and move directly to the tips, I
strongly suggest that when you have more time you come back
to the crucial following information. Understanding the role
sodium plays in the body and the difference between "good"
and "bad" sources of sodium will help you get the salt out of
your diet while you still meet your sodium needs.

■ ■ ■

UNDERSTANDING SALT AND SODIUM

Sodium is essential to life.

Sodium is so important, in fact, that humans have a specific sensor on the tongue that can detect salt. Thousands of years ago, when the diet of humans was potassium-rich and sodium-poor, this sensor for salt was a crucial survival tool. Nature, in her infinite wisdom, devised a way to help humans (as well as animals) seek out salty foods so they could be assured of receiving adequate sodium from their diets. This is important because sodium—often found in the form of sodium chloride or salt—plays countless roles in the body.

To begin with, sodium is crucial for maintaining the health of every cell in the human system. It permeates the fluid between cells (often called the "extracellular fluid") and potassium exists mainly on the inside of the cells (in the "intracellular fluid"). These two minerals need to be in constant dynamic balance so nutrient and waste exchange can take place across cell membranes. If either of these minerals is deficient or in excess, cell permeability becomes compromised and the health of all our cells suffers.

Besides being a component of the extracellular fluid that bathes every living cell, sodium is important in two other "salty oceans" in the body—our blood and our lymphatic fluid. It also is necessary for the production of hydrochloric acid, the digestive enzyme secreted by the stomach in order to digest protein. Along with potassium, sodium is required for the proper functioning of our nerves and the contraction of our muscles. (The heart, as you may know, is our hardest-working muscle.) Finally, sodium is necessary to maintain several kinds of equilibrium—fluid balance, electrolyte balance, and pH (acid/alkaline) balance—which are all of utmost importance to the body.

With the many crucial roles sodium plays, it's clear that if we had *no* sodium, we would cease to exist. Obtaining adequate, easily absorbable sodium from foods, then, is important for maintaining health, but obtaining too much of the *wrong kinds* of sodium is harmful.

To understand why this is true, you first need to understand that humans evolved on a diet that was high in potassium and low in sodium. All unprocessed natural foods—with the exception of just a few kinds of shellfish—contain more potassium than sodium. A diet consisting exclusively of these foods caused our ancestors to consume about *ten times* more potassium than sodium, and over thousands of years, the human body developed mechanisms so that it could survive and actually thrive under these dietary conditions. Since potassium was abundant at every meal, the human body adapted by learning that it did not need to retain much potassium and could, in a sense, afford to waste it.

Sodium, on the other hand, was a different story. Because the sodium content of the Paleolithic diet was quite low, the human body developed a taste for salt just to ensure adequate sodium intake. In addition, the body became adept at absorbing sodium and conserving every precious milligram it consumed. This function continues today, even though the standard American diet is now low in potassium and exceedingly high in sodium. What once was an evolutionary adaptation that served humans well for tens of thousands of years is now a hazard because we have dramatically changed our diet and, consequently, our intake of these important minerals.

Simply put, the human body evolved to thrive on minimal amounts of sodium and much more potassium than sodium.

Today, however, because we are faced with a growing number of environmental, emotional, and psychological stresses, many of us actually require more sodium than our Paleolithic ancestors consumed. Although few people realize it, sodium plays a key role in our body's ability to adapt to stress (which I will explain later in this preface in the section How Much Sodium Do We Need?). For that reason, I recommend that most individuals consume about 2,000 milligrams of sodium a day —an amount still far below the typical American's intake and well within the FDA's current guidelines. This recommendation is a general rule of thumb; remember that individual requirements vary based on many factors.

As you have read, adequate sodium is tremendously important to our health. Equally as important, however, is the *kind* of sodium we consume. Just as there are "good" fats and "bad" fats, so, too, there are "good" sodium sources and "bad" sodium sources. As you might guess, sodium that occurs naturally in foods is good, but commercial table salt is bad. It bears repeating that refined salt is a harmful source of sodium that the body needs to detoxify rather than a source the body can readily use.

Commercial refined salt is not only stripped of all its minerals besides sodium and chloride, but it also is heated at such high temperatures that the chemical structure of salt changes. In addition, it is chemically cleaned and bleached and treated with anticaking agents, which prevent salt from mixing with water in the salt container. Unfortunately, the anticaking agents perform the same function in the human body, so refined salt does not dissolve and combine with the water and fluids present in our system. Instead, it builds up in the body and leaves deposits in organs and tissue, causing severe health problems.

Two of the most common anticaking agents used in the mass production of salt are sodium alumino-silicate and alumino-calcium silicate. These are both sources of aluminum, a toxic metal that has been implicated in the development of Alzheimer's disease and that certainly does not belong in a healthy diet. To make matters worse, the aluminum used in salt production leaves a bitter taste in salt, so manufacturers usually add sugar in the form of dextrose to hide the taste of the aluminum. Refined sugar—as I explained in my previous book, *Get the Sugar Out* (Harmony Books, 1996)—severely disrupts the equilibrium of the body and is associated with the development of more than sixty diseases.

Whether you consider the minerally unbalanced condition of the salt we use, the anticaking agents that prevent salt from doing some of its most important jobs in the body, or the chemicals and sugar that are added to it, table salt should be avoided because it is, without a doubt, hazardous to human health. The next section will show you just what kinds of health problems refined salt can cause.

THE PROBLEMS WITH SALT AND SODIUM

Current research is uncovering dozens of connections between disease and excess use of salt, but hypertension remains the most serious, the most prevalent, and the most recognized condition associated with a high intake of salt.

HYPERTENSION Hypertension, which is defined as consistent blood pressure readings above 140/90, affects about one in every four adults, making it the most common medical problem in the United States today. High blood pressure is especially dangerous because it is a "silent killer." It can cause tissue damage for up to twenty years before any discernible symptoms arise, and all too often, people become aware of their condition only when they suddenly and unexpectedly suffer one of the often life-threatening complications of hypertension:

heart attack
stroke
arteriosclerosis (hardening of the arteries)
serious kidney damage or kidney failure
bleeding in the eyes, impaired sight, or blindness
enlarged heart
congestive heart failure

With devastating consequences like these, we should do everything in our power to prevent or control high blood pressure. Cutting back on salt is one of the easiest things we can do. Over the last fifty years, exhaustive research from both animal studies and human epidemiological studies (those that compare populations and their incidence of disease) support the salt-hypertension connection. Here are some highlights of that research:

No other animal besides man develops high blood pressure in its natural habit. By 1953, however, scientists found that mice, kangaroo rats, albino rats, rabbits, dogs, and cows all develop high blood pressure if they eat a lot of salt.

A recent study involving chimpanzees, the species genetically closest to humans, has provided even more definitive proof that a high intake of salt can cause hypertension. In the results reported in the October 1995 issue of *Nature Medicine,* chimps ate their typical diet, which is low in sodium, until halfway through the study, when half of them received salt supplements equivalent to the amount of salt consumed by the average human. Shortly thereafter, the blood pressures of the chimps in the test group rose dramatically, but their blood pressures went back to normal when the added salt was removed.

Intersalt, a 1988 international study of more than ten thousand people in thirty-two countries, found that high blood pressure is exceedingly rare in places where the diet is low in sodium. As sodium intakes increase, however, blood pressure readings tend to rise.

The Japanese provide proof of the real-life dangers of too much sodium in the diet. They consume more sodium than the citizens of any other nation in the world: the average intake is 6,000 to 10,000 milligrams of sodium per person per day, and some residents consume as much as 20,000 milligrams. With so much sodium, the Japanese have a hypertension rate that is almost double the hypertension rate in the United States. In addition, their rate of stroke (a common consequence of high blood pressure) is the leading cause of death in their society.

Sensitivity to salt—and the high blood pressure that usually results—is partly hereditary. Not all animals fed a diet high in salt develop hypertension; those who do are often genetically predisposed to the disease. In the late 1950s, though, researcher Lewis K. Dahl found that a diet low in salt could keep rats free of hypertension *even in rats that were genetically programmed to develop it.*

Subsequent studies on humans have shown that lowering sodium intake does not always lower blood pressure in hypertensive patients, but it does so in about half of the people who have the condition.

Part of the problem with identifying the true relationship between sodium and hypertension is that many factors besides sodium play a part in the development of the condition. Other contributing factors to hypertension include:

Heredity (whether one or both parents had
hypertension or were salt-sensitive)
Being a male or being a female past menopause
Excessive consumption of alcohol
Smoking
Obesity
Lack of physical exercise
Stress
Arteriosclerosis (hardening of the arteries)
Insulin resistance or elevated blood glucose levels
Excessive sugar and nonessential fat intake
Deficiencies of potassium, magnesium, and calcium

The last factor is not understood well by the American public, but it is particularly interesting. Recent research shows that obtaining adequate potassium, magnesium, and calcium may be as significant for blood pressure prevention and control as lowering salt consumption. The typical American diet is as *high* in sodium as it is *low* in these other essential nutrients. The Joint National Committee on Detection, Evaluation and Treatment of High Blood Pressure now admits that potassium, magnesium, and calcium play a role in reducing the risk of high blood pressure. Numerous studies have revealed that these often-overlooked minerals not only help lower blood pressure but they also prevent heart attacks. Therefore, it is important to realize that while reducing sodium intake is crucial for the prevention and treatment of hypertension (especially for salt-sensitive individuals), other dietary and lifestyle factors also need to be considered. The evidence against salt and sodium is certainly convincing enough to warrant a consensus among health organizations and nutrition experts that our intake should be reduced.

CALCIUM DEFICIENCY AND OSTEOPOROSIS Too much dietary sodium also increases the risk for osteoporosis and probably for kidney stones as well. Excess sodium causes calcium to be lost from the body through the urine, and then the blood level of calcium falls. The hormone system then responds to low levels of calcium in the blood by prompting the withdrawal of calcium from the bones. A study reported in the June 1995 *Journal of Human Hypertension* confirms that when more sodium is ingested than we need, there is a rise in urine hydroxyproline levels—which indicates that bone is being broken down.

FLUID RETENTION, WEIGHT GAIN, AND HEAD-ACHES Excessive sodium causes fluid retention, which stresses the heart and circulatory system and results in edema—swelling of tissues. Edema can manifest itself in tissue puffiness or bloating all over the body or it can be localized in such areas as the ankles, fingers, pelvic, and abdominal areas. Women with hormonal problems seem to be particularly susceptible to developing fluid retention and often can become irritable or depressed when they retain water during their premenstrual cycles. Some women have been known to gain as much as fifteen pounds in "water weight" for a few days every month. Although water weight gain is not the same as fat gain, women who suffer from it temporarily have trouble fitting into their clothes and almost always can benefit from reducing their salt intake.

Fluid retention probably also contributes to two other ailments associated with excessive salt use: headaches and migraines. Although it is unknown exactly how salt does its damage, Seymour Diamond, M.D., executive director of the Diamond Headache Clinic in Chicago, has found that patients often develop headaches a few hours after eating salty food. Although Dr. Diamond has focused on salt alone, other high-sodium food additives like monosodium glutamate (MSG), sodium sulfites, nitrites, and nitrates also can trigger headaches.

STOMACH ULCERS AND STOMACH CANCER The stomach, which uses sodium to produce hydrochloric acid, seems to be particularly sensitive to unnatural, refined sources of sodium: excess salt contributes to the development of ulcers, and certain sodium additives can cause stomach cancer.

Amnon Sonnenberg, M.D., of Harvard Medical School, has seen a strong correlation between the incidence of gastric ulcers and the consumption of common (refined) table salt. According to Dr. Sonnenberg, the rise and fall of ulcers directly parallels the rise and fall of salt intake.

In addition, a high intake of salt-preserved, smoked, and cured foods is a known risk factor for stomach and esophageal cancer. The sodium nitrites and nitrates used in these foods can form nitrosamines in the stomach. These chemicals are some of the most potent cancer-causing agents known. The Japanese, who have the highest incidence of stomach ulcers and stomach cancers in the world, consume more salt-, nitrite-, and nitrate-treated foods than any other culture.

The evidence clearly shows that too much dietary sodium is a culprit in many health problems. But how much is too much? The amount actually differs from one individual to the next. The next section will help you understand why and will show you how to determine the right amount of sodium for *you*.

HOW MUCH SODIUM DO WE NEED?

The answer to "How much sodium do we need?" really depends on who you are.

Not only do your sodium needs vary depending on your genetic background, but they also change during different stages of your life, depending on such factors as how much you exercise, where you live, and what you eat.

While many health professionals today would like us to believe that all individuals can thrive on an extremely strict low-sodium diet, the issue is not nearly so black and white. There is great variance in our sodium needs and even in our tolerance to unrefined salt. If we learn about the factors that influence our sodium needs, each of us will be able to determine our individual ideal sodium intake.

GENETIC HERITAGE The genetic blueprint each of us has inherited plays a significant but greatly overlooked role in many aspects of nutrition and body chemistry. In no area is that more apparent than in our varying reactions to salt.

Officially, about half of all people who have high blood pressure—and a quarter of people who have normal blood pressure—are considered "salt-sensitive," but many of us are salt-sensitive to one degree or another. Very salt-sensitive individuals experience troublesome symptoms like water retention or an increase in blood pressure when they use even the slightest amount of salt. Less salt-sensitive people, probably the majority of us, can tolerate moderate amounts of sodium, while a few individuals can consume large amounts of sodium without experiencing health problems. These individuals appear to be salt-resistant. (Some, however, have argued that even in these individuals, a long-term diet high in salt can "set the stage" for high blood pressure and other illnesses later on in life.)

Salt-sensitivity runs along family lines: if one or both parents are salt-sensitive, their children are much more likely to be salt-sensitive, too. But our salt-sensitivity—and our particular requirements for sodium—are also influenced by ancestors a bit further back in our history. As I explained in my book *Your Body Knows Best* (Pocket Books, 1996), scientific researchers have discovered that our nutrient needs are determined far more by where our ancestors originated than by where we live now.

This fact seems particularly evident in the case of blacks, who are more salt-sensitive than whites and have a higher incidence of hypertension. Most blacks or their ancestors originally lived in warm tropical climates where very-low-sodium, high-potassium fresh fruits, vegetables, and other plant foods were abundant, and their body chemistries adapted to these native foods and dietary conditions. Even though many blacks today have moved away from the lands of their distant ancestors, they continue to carry in their genes a sodium-sparing mechanism and greater need for potassium. This makes the high-sodium, low-potassium standard American diet (often called S.A.D.) particularly problematic and dangerous for African Americans. Statistics prove this. The American Heart Association reports that compared to whites, blacks have a greater rate of deaths from stroke, heart disease, and kidney failure, and high blood pressure is the number-one preventable cause of more than sixty-five thousand deaths annually among African Americans.

This is only one way genetic background affects our sodium requirements. Further research will likely uncover other similar correlations in the future.

STRESS Another factor that can greatly affect our tolerance to salt is the amount of stress we experience and how we react to it. When the human body experiences any type of stress—whether it is physical, emotional, or psychological—the body responds in the following ways:

STAGE 1: THE ALARM REACTION. During the beginning stage of stress (which is often called the "fight or flight syndrome"), the adrenal glands, the body's "stress glands," produce extra amounts of adrenal hormones to help the body mobilize its energy to meet the stress. Blood pressure rises, heartbeat increases, sugar is mobilized from the liver, and the adrenals overproduce aldosterone, a hormone that causes the kidneys to retain sodium in the body. People who are in this stage of stress may not even consume much sodium in their diet, but they *retain salt in their tissues* because of their stressed body chemistry. (Note: if the source of stress is removed, the adrenals return to their normal functioning and sodium levels also return to normal.)

STAGE 2: THE RESISTANCE STAGE. Gradually, if the stress continues over a long period of time, the body enters a stage of resistance in which it requires nutrients in excess of its normal needs. To meet its additional requirements, the body draws on vitamins and minerals from its tissue reserves.

STAGE 3: THE EXHAUSTION STAGE. If the stress continues for too long, the body eventually uses up its reserves of both energy and nutrients and falls into a state of exhaustion. During this stage, the body's adrenal glands become burned out and no longer have the ability to produce aldosterone. Without enough aldosterone, the body loses sodium through the urine and actually becomes *deficient in sodium*—not because it consumes too little sodium but because it cannot hold on to the sodium it absorbs.

In my nutritional practice, I see many clients who have elevated blood and tissue sodium levels. These individuals are developing problems like high blood pressure, edema, or kidney disease. Today, however, as a sign of our stressful times, I am seeing an increasing number—the majority of my clients, in fact—who have low sodium levels because of weakened adrenal glands. These individuals oftentimes are allergic, suffer from chronic fatigue, experience tremendous flatulence, have low blood pressure, and have cold hands and feet.

Individuals in this stage of stress can benefit from a temporary increase in sodium intake until their adrenal glands can be strengthened. On the other hand, individuals in the initial alarm stage of stress can be helped by reducing sources of unnecessary sodium in their diet until their body chemistry improves. (For more information on nutritional ways to strengthen adrenal glands and normalize body chemistry, see the sections Dealing with Stress and Nutrient Necessities sections in chapter 10.)

GET TESTED One way to determine how much sodium you may need is by asking your doctor to perform a simple nutrient analysis blood test on you. If your sodium level falls between 137 and 144, you probably will do best with moderate levels of sodium in your diet (about 2,000 milligrams a day). If you have a sodium blood level above 144, you are retaining salt in your tissues and need to eliminate unnecessary sodium sources, especially sources like salt-contaminated water. (See chapter 2 for more information on this common problem.) If you have a sodium level below 137, you have low sodium and may need to increase your sodium intake slightly.

OTHER FACTORS Other factors can affect whether we need more or less sodium in our diets:

> **Age.** People become more salt- and sodium-sensitive as they age. (Some experts believe that the development of

both salt-sensitivity and hypertension in middle age would decrease dramatically if we consumed less sodium throughout our lifetimes.)

Weight. Overweight individuals generally are more sensitive to salt than individuals who are of average weight.

Disease. Individuals who have kidney damage or renal disease are less able to tolerate salt and excessive sodium than healthy individuals.

Environment. Individuals who live in high elevations need more sodium than those who live in lower altitudes.

Exercise and physical activity. Individuals who exercise frequently or work in physically strenuous jobs require more sodium than others. Endurance athletes, in particular, lose large quantities of sodium through perspiration and need to be especially careful to replenish sodium and other electrolytes.

Illness or accident. During a bout with the flu or any type of illness that includes repeated vomiting or diarrhea, sodium can become depleted in the body and should be replaced. This same situation can occur in any type of accident where bleeding has occurred.

Diet. Vegetarians, who consume much more potassium than sodium from plant foods, often need to add some naturally rich sodium sources or unrefined salt to their diet to better balance these two important electrolytes.

Pregnancy. Pregnant women require more sodium to accommodate the sodium needs of the growing fetus. Care should be taken to eat additional nutrient-dense foods to meet the extra requirements for sodium and other nutrients. However, to prevent the development of pregnancy-induced hypertension (PIH), pregnant women need to avoid high-salt junk foods and be sure they are getting enough protein, calories, and calcium.

As this section has shown you, sodium needs vary widely from one individual to the next. Giving a blanket nutritional prescription for people who have so many various lifestyles and different genetic backgrounds is an invitation to trouble for our individual and collective health. The answer to our individual sodium requirements isn't as simple as some experts would like us to believe. The truth is that some of us require more sodium and some of us require less, but all of us can benefit from getting refined salt out of our diets.

SO WHAT DO WE EAT?

Getting the refined salt out of our diets and reducing our sodium intake to a more moderate level requires only one main strategy: to eat as naturally as possible.

It may sound simplistic, but it's true: *natural foods are always lower in sodium than their processed and packaged counterparts.* What is the difference between processed and natural foods? Processed foods usually come packaged in boxes, plastic bags, and cans, and are designed to sit on grocery shelves for months. Healthful, natural foods, on the other hand, are as close to their natural state as possible. They include:

Vegetables	Fish
Whole grains	Shellfish
Legumes	Poultry
Nuts	Eggs
Seeds	Milk
Fruits	Lean meats

All of these foods have no refined salt and all of them, except for shellfish like lobster, shrimp, and crab, are low in sodium. Shellfish, however, can be included in a low- to moderate-sodium diet because they are sources of "good" sodium, which the body can easily use, as well as sources of other important minerals. Natural foods have other benefits, too: ounce for ounce, they contain considerably more of the essential nutrients humans require than processed foods do. They are particularly rich in potassium, a mineral that balances the action of sodium in the body, and many are good sources of magnesium and calcium as well. Potassium, magnesium, and calcium are all believed to counteract the effects of excess sodium in the diet and help prevent conditions like high blood pressure and heart disease.

Once you emphasize natural foods in your diet, refined salt no longer will be a problem. In fact, low-sodium eating will come about automatically. All you have to do is combine natural foods in any way you see fit and—*voilà!*—both unhealthy forms of sodium and excessive sodium in general will go by the wayside.

The only other thing you will need to do is fine tune your diet to find the balance of protein, carbohydrates, and fats that's right for you. Some of us seem to thrive on higher amounts of complex carbohydrates while others are actually better designed for more protein and high-quality fats. (If this concept seems strange to you, think about the Eskimos, who eat large amounts of meat and fatty fish and practically no produce but are quite healthy.) Most of us, however, do well with an almost equal balance in our diets: protein from both animal and vegetable sources; complex carbohydrates from fresh vegetables, fruits, whole grains, and legumes; and essential fats from nuts, seeds, and unrefined vegetable oils. Be sure to experiment with your natural foods diet to determine the ideal amount of each of these three nutrients for you.

No matter which balance of nutrients suits you best, natural foods will cause your sodium intake to drop so dramatically that you can afford to use small amounts of salty seasonings such as natural cheese or reduced-sodium tamari soy sauce as condiments. You'll even be able to add some "good" salt—either unrefined sea salt or a rock salt called Real Salt—at the table. (See the section Healthier Salts and Salternatives in chapter 1 for more information on these products.) Although salting food at the table may seem contradictory to the theme of the book, statistics clearly show that it is not. *Ninety percent of the sodium Americans consume comes from processed and prepared foods;* only 5 percent comes from the use of the salt shaker after cooking. Research also shows that salt added after cooking tastes stronger than when it is added before or during cooking. This means that by adding salt at the table instead of during the preparation of food, you will be apt to use less. Therefore, if you drastically cut down on both processed foods and salt used in cooking, you can feel free to add a few dashes of natural salt to foods. It will help you meet your sodium requirements and will satisfy your taste for salt far more than the salt that is hidden in greater quantities in processed foods. A little bit of salt is all you need though, as the following chart will show you:

$1/8$ teaspoon natural salt = 250 milligrams sodium
$1/4$ teaspoon natural salt = 500 milligrams sodium
$1/2$ teaspoon natural salt = 1,000 milligrams sodium
$3/4$ teaspoon natural salt = 1,500 milligrams sodium
1 teaspoon natural salt = 2,000 milligrams sodium

A misconception about salt is the belief that we need to use salt that is iodized. (Iodine, as you may know, is an essential mineral that promotes the proper functioning of the thyroid gland.) Although table salt, which is stripped of all its minerals, has iodide added to it to ensure adequate intake, both unrefined sea salt and Real Salt contain trace amounts of naturally occurring iodine. If you use natural salt as recommended in this book and eat iodine-rich fish or seafood, or use seaweed-based salt substitutes at least a few times a week, you can rest assured that your iodine intake will more than meet your needs. (See tips 54, 55, 60, and 61 for more information on iodine-containing salts and salt substitutes.)

The taste for salt is one of four basic, instinctive tastes humans have, but the manner in which we satisfy that taste is a learned behavior. Unfortunately, most Americans have been conditioned to indulge their taste for salt with poor quality foods, especially nutrient-poor refined carbohydrates, that are only given some semblance of taste with killer doses of refined salt—something cookbook author Jeanne Jones calls "the great dietary whitewash."

Instead of continually spiking the foods you eat with more and more salt, use this book to stimulate other long-ignored tastes, to accentuate your sense of smell, and to satisfy your taste for salt naturally and intelligently. Doing so will show you how to enjoy real foods again and how to create meals that both your taste buds and your body can truly savor.

USING THIS BOOK

Contrary to popular belief, getting the salt out of your diet isn't as simple as passing up the use of the salt shaker.

In fact, if you're the average American, throwing away your salt shaker will hardly make a dent in your sodium intake because salt added at the table is minimal compared to the salt that is hidden in the processed foods we eat every day. Salt is added so insidiously and so routinely to foods by manufacturers that it's difficult to escape it. From obviously salted snack foods like chips, pretzels, and roasted party nuts to basic staples like soups and breads, salt is in there. It's even hidden in cereals like cornflakes and desserts like instant chocolate pudding.

The use of salt in the cooking and processing of foods is so widespread that getting the salt out clearly requires a multidimensional approach. It means developing a "salt savvy"—learning where salt normally is found and how to do without it creatively and tastefully.

The tips in this book will help you do exactly that, but you may not be willing or able to try every suggestion. Remember that the tips were written to give helpful hints for people wanting to slightly reduce their sodium intake as well as for salt-sensitive individuals who need to severely restrict their sodium intake—and everyone in between. Just begin using the tips that seem most helpful and appealing to you, and your success with those tips may motivate you to try others in the future. Even if you use only one-tenth of the tips in the book, you'll almost certainly reduce the salt in your diet in a significantly healthy way.

To help you in your quest to get the salt out of your diet, I have marked tips throughout this book with *Salt Shaker* ratings, ranging from one to three. (Tips without a *Salt Shaker* rating don't require one. They are simply general concepts you need to understand to help you develop your salt savvy.)

One Salt Shaker refers to tips and recipes that contain healthy sodium that totals *140 milligrams or less per serving.* This includes all foods that are labeled "sodium free," "very low sodium," and "low sodium." It also distinguishes recipes that are low in salt as well as those that contain no added salt, salt-containing condiments, or salty ingredients. The recipes in this category use only unrefined whole foods, contain more potassium than sodium (as virtually all natural foods do), and should be safe for very salt-sensitive individuals and those on low-sodium diets.

The *Two Salt Shakers* ranking is given to foods that contain *between 140 milligrams and 250 milligrams of sodium per serving.* This includes sodium-rich natural foods like crab, and recipes that contain small amounts of added salt or salty processed ingredients like cheese. These foods usually are well tolerated by most healthy adults who are on prevention-oriented, health maintenance diets.

Foods labeled with *Three Salt Shakers* provide *more than 250 milligrams of sodium (or 1/8 teaspoon of salt) per serving.* Recipes with this ranking are quite high in sodium, but they offer a superior alternative to the usual high-sodium fare because they supply natural sources of sodium instead of refined salt *or* because they contain high amounts of potassium and other minerals that negate some of the hazardous effects of a high-sodium intake. Tips designated with *Three Salt Shakers* can be used as beginning steps when you feel that you're addicted to salt and are trying to cut down. They also can be used for occasional "splurges" when your diet as a whole is low in sodium. If you have trouble reducing the salt in your diet, eating foods designated with *Three Salt Shakers* is a great place to start. Remember, though, that eating these foods alone will not reduce your sodium intake enough to be within the FDA's recommended maximum daily quantity of 2,400 milligrams of sodium. To keep your sodium intake within these guidelines, at least be sure to balance your intake of *One, Two,* and *Three Salt Shaker* foods.

Although some of us may not be able to enjoy our best health on an extremely strict low-sodium diet, this book still emphasizes *One Salt Shaker* tips and recipes. This is because you can salt according to your individual needs and tastes at the table and easily change *One Salt Shaker* into *Two* or *Three Salt Shakers* if needed. If you add slightly more than $1/16$ of a teaspoon of salt per serving to a *One Salt Shaker* recipe, it will become a *Two Salt Shaker* recipe; $1/8$ of a teaspoon of salt per serving changes the recipe into *Three Salt Shakers*.

How much salt you should add to foods will depend on such things as your salt sensitivity, your unique sodium needs, and how well you eliminate processed foods and salt used in cooking. If you're concerned about adding natural salt at the table, you need to understand that while sodium needs do vary, reducing sodium too much can be just as harmful as consuming large amounts of it. Too little sodium can cause spasms, poor heart rhythm, and sudden death. A study reported on in the June 1995 issue of *Hypertension* found that hypertensive patients who consumed the lowest sodium intake were actually four times more likely to have heart attacks than other participants in the study. *Low salt, not no salt, appears to be best as a permanent way of eating for most individuals.*

Of course, you should receive most of the sodium to meet your requirements from natural foods. Just a shake or two of salt added to foods usually is all most of us need or want. As you gradually get the salt out of your diet, your tastes will change. You'll be able to discern many subtle flavors that you used to miss completely, and you'll begin to enjoy and prefer low-salt food after a short adaptation period of just two to eight weeks. When you use the flavorful cooking tips in this book, meals will no longer overemphasize the salty taste alone, but instead they will be transformed into whole new adventures in taste and aroma. You'll also find that you have a great deal of freedom in the variety of meals you can eat when you reduce your sodium intake. You can have most of the foods that you thought were forbidden—nachos, sausage, and even pickles—as long as you prepare those foods with salt savvy.

In addition to the 501 tips that will help you develop your salt savvy, this book also includes Bonus Tips, which are not specifically about getting the refined salt out of your diet. They will, however, make things easier in the kitchen, add to your nutritional knowledge, and help you to be a smarter food consumer in general.

Throughout *Get the Salt Out*, I refer to other books both as sources of recipes and as references for related topics. Learning how and why to cook without salt are complex subjects, so you may want to refer to these books for more detailed information on specific topics of interest to you. A list of the books appears in the bibliography at the back of this book.

In addition to the books, I also mention specific brands of products that can be helpful when trying to stick to a low- to moderate-sodium diet. The products I have mentioned can provide quick convenience without the salt that normally accompanies prepared foods. Although the emphasis in the diet always should be to eat as many fresh, natural foods as possible, it's important to understand that packaged and convenience food products can be used as long as you select them carefully.

As I explained in the Preface, sodium requirements and salt sensitivity vary from individual to individual. Some of us are extremely sensitive to the tiniest bit of salt, while others seem to be able to handle large amounts. Even if salt doesn't seem to be a problem right now for you, remember all the evidence showing that long-term overconsumption of salt takes a serious toll on the body. Most Americans would benefit by reducing sodium intake by at least half.

How far you go in your quest to reduce your use of salt is entirely up to you. It will depend on your individual biochemistry, your present health condition, and how well you develop your salt savvy. Whatever your long-term sodium-reduction and health goals are, make sure to celebrate each successful step that you make toward achieving them.

Incidentally, although you may not realize it, the fact that you are reading this book means that you already have taken your first step. You have decided to pay attention to the scientific evidence about salt and sodium and put that knowledge into action to improve your health. Congratulations and good luck on your new adventure!

GET THE SALT OUT

CHAPTER 1

Get the Salt Out
of Your Kitchen

Many salt-reducing tips are versatile. Once you learn them, you can use them when making anything from breakfast to party foods. They can be utilized repeatedly, anywhere and anytime, until they become habits and maybe even family traditions.

The tips in this chapter are your beginning lessons, and they should become your mainstays. They are fundamental ways to break the salt habit—basic concepts that will teach you how to limit, substitute, or eliminate salt in the foods you put in your shopping cart, the foods you have in your kitchen, and the way you prepare food.

Begin by remembering the concepts and using the tips that seem most simple and appealing to you. Once those tips become second nature, try using other suggestions that seem more unfamiliar to you.

Making lifestyle changes is never easy, but it's particularly difficult to change dietary habits that have been ingrained since childhood. The liberal use of salt is automatic for most Americans. Breaking this habit usually has to be a gradual process, and it's best to proceed at your own pace.

It also helps when you know exactly how and why you

should get the salt out of your diet. The tips in this chapter cover those important hows and whys and serve as the foundation for all of the other tips in this book. Get to know this chapter well and keep reminding yourself that the efforts you make today will pay off in rewards to your health in the future.

TOP TEN TIPS

1 ▪ Avoid processed foods as much as possible. Products that come in boxes, packages, and cans are designed for a long shelf life and are the number-one source of salt in our diets. In addition, they frequently contain sodium additives and preservatives, sugar and hydrogenated fats, all of which are known to cause health problems. For all of these reasons, your top priority in getting the salt out should be to eliminate these refined, fake foods.

2 ▪ Think fresh and natural. Nature designed foods that are perfect for us —low in sodium but otherwise filled with nutrients. Fresh plant foods and unprocessed animal foods fit this description; all others don't. Therefore, choosing foods low in sodium is relatively easy: when in doubt, opt for the more natural food choice.

3 ▪ Substitute unrefined sea salt or Real Salt for common table salt in your salt shaker. Remember: the *kind* of salt you use is just as important as the amount of salt you use. Common table salt is harmful; it doesn't dissolve in the body and tends to build up. Unrefined sea salt and Real Salt, however, are "good" salts the body can easily use for the many roles sodium plays. See Resources in the back of the book for information on where you can purchase Real Salt.

4 ▪ **Use only the amount of salt that is right for you.** Sensitivity to salt, even to "good" kinds of salt, is an individual response. Some of us can tolerate moderate amounts easily, while others do much better with very little. Add the amount that is right for you. At home, have each family member salt his or her own food.

5 ▪ **Eliminate, or at least reduce, the amount of salt used in cooking.** Salt added during the cooking of foods accounts for a big chunk of the sodium we consume: 45 percent. It also is not tasted as well by our taste buds as salt that is added to foods after cooking. Therefore, feel free to use natural salt at the table (which accounts for only 5 percent of our sodium intake), but try to eliminate salt and salt-containing ingredients from your recipes.

6 ▪ **Become a consumer-savvy food detective:** seek out products that are low in sodium or have no salt added. An unsalted product used in place of a regularly salted ingredient often can reduce your sodium intake by hundreds, sometimes even a thousand milligrams, in one meal alone!

7 ▪ **Make your meals come alive with savory salt-free seasonings** like garlic, herbs, and spices. If you use these seasonings in your cooking, then eating can become such a flavorful experience that you'll never even miss the salt.

8 ▪ **Use naturally salty nutritious foods like unprocessed cheese and reduced-sodium tamari (see tip 63) in small amounts.** When your diet as a whole is low in sodium, you can afford small amounts of salty natural foods in your diet for flavor. Remember to think of these foods as condiments though: a little bit of them can go a long way.

9 ▪ **Emphasize the K factor at every meal.** K is the chemical symbol for potassium, a mineral that counteracts the effects of too much sodium in the diet. It is known to protect against hypertension, strokes, and heart disease. All natural foods contain potassium, but fresh vegetables and fruits contain the most. Therefore, in keeping with the National Cancer Institute's "Five a Day" campaign, try to have at least five servings of vegetables and fruits each day.

10 ▪ **Eat for taste *and* good nutrition,** not just taste alone. Remember, our taste for salt has far exceeded our need. Food manufacturers and restaurants, in fact, frequently take advantage of the human taste for salt, making profits off the sales of poor-quality, nutrient-deficient but heavily salted foods we otherwise would not eat. It's important to remember that your taste for salt can lessen, but your fundamental requirements for nutrients have to be met each and every day. They simply can't be met by a diet high in salty processed foods.

TRICKS OF THE TRADE

11 ▪ **Do not eliminate salt cold turkey.** Getting the salt out of your diet too fast and too drastically can stress the heart and be harmful. Better to substitute unrefined forms of salt for common table salt and . . .

12 ▪ **Gradually cut the salt you use in cooking.** First, try reducing the salt in a recipe by one-quarter or one-half. Continue to reduce the salt each time you make the recipe until you eventually use little or no salt in cooking.

13 ▪ **Add salt to foods *after* cooking for better flavor.** Salt added before or during cooking never tastes as salty as salt that is added after cooking. The flavor dissipates in the cooking process. Make the salt you *do* use go further by adding it later.

14 ▪ **If you crave salt,** it's a likely sign that your adrenal glands, which help you deal with stress, are tuckered out. That's at least what Douglas Hunt, M.D., says in his book *No More Cravings* (Warner Books, 1987). If "stressed out" sounds like you, you need to strengthen those adrenal glands by being especially good to yourself, learning to relax, and paying particular attention to the tips in the sections Nutrient Necessities and Dealing with Stress in chapter 10. (This advice can't hurt even if you don't have weakened adrenals.)

15 ▪ **According to Chinese medicine, salt cravings** can be the body's attempt to balance too much sugar or alcohol in the diet. Cut down on sugar and alcohol to make it easier for you to get the salt out of your diet and to improve your health in general.

16 ▪ **An exaggerated appetite for salt** can sometimes be a symptom of impending hypertension as well as an important contributing factor. Have your blood pressure checked regularly no matter what you eat, but especially if you can't seem to taste salt well and tend to use lots of it on your food.

17 ▪ **Be sure to get enough sleep and rest.** This is a simple but frequently forgotten prescription for health that can make reducing salt in the diet much easier. It also can help hold salt cravings at bay. You see, when your body is tired, it wants energy. Salt can temporarily increase the metabolism of a tired body, which is why you may crave or even binge on salty foods when you're fatigued. Unfortunately though, salt does not correct the exhaustion you may feel. The only solution is to give your body proper, balanced nourishment and adequate rest.

18 ▪ **Eat more meals at home,** where you can oversee the ingredients. When you make simply prepared meals at home, you can avoid the unnecessary salt and sodium that are often hidden in restaurant food.

19 ▪ **Remember this: a liking for salty food is one of the easiest eating habits to get over.** According to Andrew Weil, M.D., author of *Natural Health, Natural Medicine* (Houghton

Mifflin Company, 1990), reducing salt in the diet is much easier to do than reducing fat or sugar. Dr. Weil says that many humans have a "fat tooth" in addition to a sweet tooth as a legacy of evolution, but our liking for high amounts of salt is a learned behavior that we can easily unlearn.

TOOLS OF THE TRADE

20 ▪ Buy a set of good, sharp knives to facilitate easy slicing and dicing of fresh ingredients. When you're venturing into low-salt cooking, the last thing you want is frustration during food preparation because your knives are more of a hindrance to you than a help. Appetizing low-salt cooking largely depends on using abundant, flavorful, chopped fresh produce, so purchase the best set of knives that you can.

21 ▪ Or get a food processor to make food preparation even easier. Whether you need to chop, grate, puree, or blend, a food processor will help you do the work in virtually no time.

22 ▪ A blender is also a handy tool for whipping up quick vegetable- and herb-based sauces and salad dressings that are so tasty you'll forget all about the salt-laden instant varieties.

23 ▪ Try using waterless cookware, the cookware I use. Waterless cookware will help you get not only the salt out of the foods you cook, it will help you get the sugar and fat out as well. The cookware's amazing design allows food to cook in its own juices at a constant 180 degrees—the temperature that kills off *E. coli,* salmonella, and other unwanted microorganisms but allows all of the vitamins, minerals, and natural flavors to remain. To cook the most delicious and easiest salt-free foods you've ever tasted, treat yourself to a Royal Prestige cooking set.

To order or to get more information, call Uni Key, which is listed in the Resources section.

24 ▪ **A wide-mouthed thermos** is helpful for taking low-sodium soups, stews, and leftovers to work with you. When you have warm soup from home all ready to eat, you have instant fast food that's both economical and healthful.

25 ▪ **Invest in a good pepper mill.** Fresh-ground pepper always perks up salt-free food more than preground pepper.

▪ BONUS TIP: *According to Paul Pitchford, author of* Healing with Whole Foods *(North Atlantic Books, 1993), freshly ground pepper is more desirable than commercial ground pepper for another reason: commercial ground pepper is roasted, a process that makes the pepper become an irritant to the system. When you grind whole fresh peppercorns in a pepper mill, you avoid this problem.*

26 ▪ **Consider getting a spice grinder,** a small, hand-turned mill that allows you to make freshly ground herb seeds, spices, and seasoning blends of all types. Remember: the fresher the flavor in your food, the less you'll miss salt.

27 ▪ **Speaking of flavor, a mortar and pestle** are musts for bringing out the peak taste and aroma of herbs and spices. It takes slightly more time to crush herbs and spices than to use ready-made ground seasonings, but the extra flavor can't be beat.

TASTEFUL TECHNIQUES

28 ▪ **Learn to enjoy the taste of foods as they are,** without any added salt. If you lessen salt in your diet gradually, you'll be amazed to find that foods you ate regularly a month or two ago suddenly seem much too salty. Even more encouraging, you'll find that natural foods that seemed bland before are really delicious. Studies conducted at the Monell Chemical Senses Center confirm that people's desire for salt falls off as they use less of it.

29 ▪ Explore the five tastes. This is a tip that not only will make eating more pleasurable, but may actually improve your health as well. According to the ancient Five Element Theory of food therapy in Chinese medicine, too much of one taste can cause imbalance in the body. Most Americans overindulge the sweet and salty tastes and don't appreciate the other equally important tastes: sour (as in a lemon); bitter (as in mustard greens); and pungent (as in a radish). Emphasize these other tastes to establish better balance in your diet and your health.

30 ▪ "Fool" your taste buds into thinking salt is present by overstimulating one of the other tastes. Jeanne Jones, a spa menu consultant and author of many low-salt cookbooks, passed this tip on to me, and it's true. This concept explains why many people can kick the salt habit when they use sour vinegar or lemon juice liberally.

31 ▪ Remember to stimulate your sense of smell because it is closely connected to your sense of taste. In fact, besides your basic tastes, all of your other "tastes" are really smells. To demonstrate this fact, Jeanne Jones recommends that you try this test: hold your nose the next time you eat one of your favorite foods. You'll probably be surprised how little you actually taste.

32 ▪ Satisfy occasional yens for salt with small amounts of foods that have salt on the surface (for example, salted nuts). The tongue's sensors can distinguish the taste of salt on the surface of foods much more quickly, easily, and potently than they can pick up the taste of salt when it is mixed or cooked into foods. (This is another reason to sprinkle a small amount on your food at the table instead of mixing salt in while you cook.)

33 ▪ Do not try to determine the sodium content of foods by relying on your taste buds. The taste buds were designed to pick up the salty taste, yet most forms of sodium (like the sodium additives in many processed foods) do not taste salty. In addition, taste buds can become confused by the combination of salt and sugar in processed foods. The salty taste and the sweet taste offset each other, which gives us an inaccurate impression that these foods contain less salt and sugar than they really do.

34 ▪ Taste food before you salt it (if you decide to salt it). This is an obvious tip too many of us forget. All too often, we grab for the salt shaker without thinking about it, even before we take one bite. Replace this unhealthy habit with a "taste and decide" approach: if a food needs natural salt, by all means add a shake or two, but go easy. You always can add more later if you need to, but it's impossible to remove salt once you've added it.

HERB MAGIC

35 ▪ Use herbs and spices imaginatively. Most of us haven't begun to explore the taste possibilities available to us through the creative use of these small gifts from nature. Herbs and spices may be small, but you'll find they can produce wonderfully big flavors. When you tantalize your taste buds with everything from hot cayenne to pungent mustard, your taste buds will be happy to experience these new flavors in place of salt.

36 ▪ Besides their taste, there's another reason to use herbs and spices in cooking: many of them are rich in nutrients that are beneficial to our health. The herb tarragon, for example, is an excellent source of potassium, a mineral that works in a seesaw balance with sodium and can counteract some of sodium's negative effects. Ounce for ounce, tiny tarragon packs a powerful nutritional punch: according to Judith Benn Hurley, author of *The Good Herb* (William Morrow and Company, 1995), one tablespoon of tarragon supplies 145 milligrams of potassium. By comparison, three ounces of potassium-rich chicken contain 195 milligrams.

37 ▪ For the best effect, use herbs and spices that are at their peak of flavor and aroma. Dried herbs and spices have a shelf life of only about six months; after that, many of them develop lifeless or unappetizing tastes. To keep their flavor as vibrant as possible you should store herbs and spices in small, airtight jars in a cool, dry, dark place away from the kitchen stove. When you open a jar of dried herbs, they should send out a fresh, strong, distinctive aroma. If they don't—if they taste more like hay than the herb they are supposed to be—you aren't utilizing the full flavoring potential of herbs. Better to discard the old batch and find some fresher herbs that will make your salt-free meals come alive.

38 ▪ If you don't use dried herbs soon after purchase, either buy them in smaller amounts or transfer some of them to a plastic bag and store them in the freezer.

39 ▪ Keep zesty ground herbs like garlic powder, onion powder, or cayenne pepper in shakers on the table. They make tasty, healthful condiments you can use in place of salt. (Be sure to buy garlic and onion *powder*, not garlic and onion *salt*.) *One Salt Shaker.*

40 ▪ Try the refreshing flavor of fresh herbs on both raw and cooked foods. Once you try them, you might just prefer the taste of fresh herbs, as I do. (To use fresh herbs in place of dried herbs in a recipe, substitute two to four times the amount of fresh herbs as the indicated amount of dried herbs.) Easy-to-find fresh herbs include basil, oregano, dill, mint, rosemary, thyme, and tarragon.

■ BONUS TIP: *If you really enjoy the flavor of fresh herbs, you might want to consider growing your own in a garden or in pots on your windowsill. It's quite a thrill to watch the herbs grow and to have ready-to-snip herbs at your fingertips.*

41 ■ **Fresh herbs can be frozen.** Whether you grow herbs yourself or find them in the produce section of your supermarket, never let fresh herbs wilt away and go bad in the refrigerator. Put the leaves, whole or chopped, in small bags and freeze them for future use. When you use them, you can add them frozen to cooked dishes; there is no need to defrost them.

42 ■ **Use the flavoring magic of herbs to make savory Herb Butter.** It's a delicious condiment that can add a gourmet touch to an everyday meal, and it has hundreds of possible uses. Try brushing fish with dill butter, topping baked potatoes with basil butter, or adding tarragon butter to steamed asparagus spears. To make Herb Butter, follow this simple recipe, which I use. *One Salt Shaker.*

■ HERB BUTTER ■

$1/2$ cup (1 stick) unsalted butter, softened to room
    temperature
$1/2$ cup finely chopped fresh herbs *or* 2 teaspoons to $1/4$
    cup crushed dried herbs

Combine both ingredients in a small bowl and mix together with a spoon until smooth and creamy. Cover tightly and chill for a few hours for the best flavor. *Makes $1/2$ cup.*

43 ■ **For fancier Herb Butter combinations,** you also can add a few teaspoons or tablespoons of salt-free tomato paste, lemon juice, wine, or vinegar to the basic recipe. *One Salt Shaker.*

44 ▪ Transform a quality olive oil into an extraordinary herbed oil through the art of infusion. Fill a one-cup glass jar with three tablespoons of fresh herbs (pounded to bruise them slightly), then add $^1/_2$ cup warmed olive oil. Allow the oil to cool, then seal the jar, and refrigerate for a few weeks before using. Fat carries the herbal flavor throughout a dish, even when you use only small amounts, so an herbed oil makes an excellent salt-free seasoning to dribble on steamed vegetables, salads, or whole-grain pasta. *One Salt Shaker.*

45 ▪ Another flavorful addition to low-salt cooking that you can make yourself is herbed vinegar. To make it, loosely fill a clean glass bottle or jar with one cup of fresh herbs of your choice. Add one quart of cider vinegar, white wine vinegar, or red wine vinegar, cap the bottle, and label it. Let it stand in a cool, dark place and after a few days, add more vinegar if needed. Cap it again, then allow the herbs to do their wonders for three to four weeks. Like an herbed oil, an herbed vinegar perks up all salt-free fare, but it's particularly good in marinades and salad dressings. *One Salt Shaker.*

46 ▪ If convenience is more important to you than price, you can purchase ready-to-use herbed vinegars and herbed oils in supermarkets. One brand of both of them that I like is Spectrum Naturals, which you can find in natural food stores nationwide. This company makes a nice assortment of flavored vinegars ranging from Italian herb wine vinegar to garlic wine vinegar to peach vinegar. All of its vinegars are made with organic grapes and contain no added sulfites, a common allergen found in commercial vinegars. Spectrum's herbed oils (called World Cuisine Oils) also are a boon for anyone trying to reduce sodium without reducing flavor. They come in five varieties that range from aromatic garlic-herb Mediterranean Oil to an Asian Oil that is a combination of fragrant sesame oil and fiery ginger and hot pepper. Just a few drops of either an herbed oil or an herbed vinegar gives surprising punch to otherwise bland food. *One Salt Shaker.*

THE PROBLEMS WITH MSG

47 ▪ **When you're looking for flavor without the salt,** you might be tempted to want to use a flavor enhancer such as monosodium glutamate (MSG). MSG can fool our taste buds into thinking foods have greater flavor than they actually do, but at an unsuspected but increasingly serious price to our health, as this section will explain.

48 ▪ **MSG excites not only the taste buds,** it also excites nerve cells, eventually damaging and killing them. Recent scientific evidence suggests that the long-term ingestion of so-called excitotoxins like MSG contributes to the development of diseases of both the brain and nervous system. As Russell L. Blaylock, M.D., says in his book *Excitotoxins: The Taste That Kills* (Health Press, 1994), "The distribution of cellular damage caused by large concentrations of MSG is very similar to that seen in human cases of Alzheimer's disease."

49 ▪ **A large and growing segment of the population** — more than 25 percent, according to MSG researcher George R. Schwartz, M.D.—reacts to the amounts of MSG that are commonly added to most processed foods today. Reactions range from mild to severe and include everything from headaches to asthma and nausea to depression. Among the most disturbing symptoms MSG can cause are chest tightness and pain, heart palpitations, and other heart irregularities. Because of serious effects like these, all of us, but especially those who have heart disease, should avoid this common but hazardous food additive.

50 ▪ **Like salt, MSG has the ability to mask inferior food quality and disguise food spoilage.** This makes MSG a nightmare for health-conscious food consumers. Restaurants and food manufacturers can use the substance to disguise unappetizing, nutrient-poor processed foods that our sense of taste would normally tell us to avoid.

51 ▪ **Naturally occurring MSG isn't the problem that synthetic MSG is.** A compound of sodium and the amino acid glutamic acid, MSG is actually found in many natural foods such as mushrooms, tomatoes, peas, and cheese. Naturally occurring MSG does not appear to cause health problems in small amounts, but isolated synthetic MSG, which is commonly added in large amounts to processed foods, clearly does.

52 ▪ **Don't forget that synthetic MSG is a source of unhealthy sodium,** and its consumption has doubled every decade since the late 1940s. Although common table salt is the number-one source of unhealthy sodium in our diet, MSG is an increasingly common—and perhaps more harmful—source. To steer clear of harmful synthetic MSG, eat as many natural foods as possible. For more tips, see the Supermarket Savvy section in this chapter and Getting What You Want and Menu Savvy in chapter 9.

HEALTHIER SALTS AND SALTERNATIVES

53 ▪ **Commercial sea salt** is better to use than common table salt because it doesn't contain the aluminum and sugar that table salt normally contains. It does, however, have many drawbacks. Like table salt, commercial sea salt is heated at high temperatures and refined to remove all naturally occurring minerals besides sodium and chloride. It also is treated with anticaking agents, but the anticaking agents used are generally less toxic than those used in table salt. When buying prepared foods, choose those that contain sea salt over those that contain salt or, better yet, buy unsalted products and season them yourself with the healthier salts listed below.

54 ▪ Unrefined sea salt is a naturally occurring salt made from evaporated seawater. To distinguish unrefined sea salt from commercial sea salt, look for a brand that is not oven dried, that contains no chemical additives, that contains naturally occurring iodine, and that has trace amounts of other minerals in addition to sodium and chloride. Unrefined sea salt also is usually slightly gray in color, and many people think it tastes saltier than table salt.

▪ BONUS TIP: *Because seawater around the world has become increasingly polluted, many health-conscious consumers have voiced concern over whether toxic chemicals may be in unrefined sea salt. I think this is a legitimate concern. For this reason, be sure to use a brand that can verify its purity.*

55 ▪ Unrefined rock salt, sold under the brand name Real Salt, is a pollutant-free salt extracted from an ancient seabed in Utah. It is not altered with any coloring, additives, or bleaching, and it is not kiln dried. It also has a full complement of trace minerals, including iodine. For all of these reasons, Real Salt is the brand of salt I recommend most often. Look for Real Salt in natural food stores throughout the country, or see the Resources section for ordering information.

56 ▪ Put the salt you now use to a test to determine its metabolic acceptability: add a spoonful to a glass of plain water, stir it several times, and let it stand overnight. If the salt collects in a thick layer on the bottom of the glass, your salt has failed the test: it is heavily processed and not very usable by the body. To give your body salt it can use, switch instead to an unrefined natural salt that will dissolve in a glass of water as well as in bodily fluids. This experiment gives you a visual example of what refined salt can do to your system: collect in body organs and clog up the circulatory system.

57 ▪ **Remember that unrefined sea or rock salt still contains 2,000 milligrams of sodium per teaspoon**—the same as common table salt. Even when the salt you use is unrefined, it should not be used with abandon. Whereas small amounts of natural salt can contribute noticeably to improved digestion, circulation, and better general well-being, too much of any salt can cause an overload of sodium in the body, increasing the likelihood of conditions like hypertension and osteoporosis. Keep this concept in mind when you begin using a healthier salt in place of table salt. Feel free to use unrefined salt; just do so in moderation.

58 ▪ **Sesame salt,** also known as gomasio, is a combination of sea salt and ground sesame seeds that is often used in macrobiotic and Oriental cooking. Since sesame seeds are good sources of important minerals like calcium, magnesium, and potassium, sesame salt is richer in minerals than unrefined sea salt by itself. It also is lower in sodium. Try some in place of salt in dishes such as bean-and-rice combinations and Chinese stir-fries.

59 ▪ **Herbal salts** are combinations of salt or sea salt and an array of tasty herbs and dehydrated vegetables. They give you a salty taste with more flavor than salt alone, and they also contain potassium and other balancing minerals that table salt simply does not have. Herbal salts are great substitutes for salt in moderate amounts, but be careful to avoid brands that contain hydrolyzed vegetable protein (HVP), autolyzed yeast, and other forms of synthetic MSG. (See tip 90 for a complete list of MSG's other names.) Two good, MSG-free herbal salts are Bioforce Herbamare and Trocomare, which can be found in health food stores. Although they contain a little more sodium than salt, they are made by curing unrefined sea salt with savory herbs and dehydrated vegetables. This process produces such a naturally flavorful herbal salt that most people who use Herbamare or Trocomare use less of it than they would salt.

60 ▪ Kelp, a seaweed, is an excellent source of iodine and sodium as well as a powerhouse of other essential minerals like potassium. This food contains potassium and sodium in a ratio of 3:1—a ratio that resembles the ratio contained in body fluids (5:1) much more closely than that of salt (1:10,000). For this reason, kelp powder and kelp flakes are used by many health enthusiasts as a salt substitute. Kelp may taste slightly fishy to some individuals, however, and it also is quite concentrated, so always use half the amount of kelp as you would salt.

61 ▪ Kombu, dulse, and other seaweeds also are rich in hard-to-find minerals of all sorts like calcium, iron, iodine, and natural sodium. You usually can find these foods in health food stores in dried sheets or strips that can be added during the cooking of foods to improve digestion and impart a naturally salty taste. Macrobiotics, a diet program that is helpful to many cancer patients, is well known for using mineral-rich foods such as grains, beans, and vegetables to provide extra flavor to normally bland soups and stocks.

62 ▪ Both soy sauce and tamari sauce are salted and fermented soy products that develop deep, rich flavors during the process of fermentation. Either one can be added to give a rich taste to Chinese stir-fries and to other foods such as Worcestershire sauce, but tamari often is the better choice because it has fewer preservatives and is less allergenic. According to *In Bad Taste: The MSG Syndrome* (Signet Books, 1990) by George R. Schwartz, M.D., tamari is lower in both salt and MSG than soy sauce, but it is not entirely MSG-free. If you use either one of these sauces, remember that they are concentrated sources of sodium—one tablespoon of either contains *about 1,000 mil-ligrams*—so use them sparingly.

63 ▪ **Reduced-sodium tamari or lite soy sauce** is a better choice of seasoning when you're getting the salt out of your diet. Both are less concentrated than regular soy sauce: depending on the brand, they can contain anywhere from 50 to 75 percent of the standard levels of sodium. The lowest-sodium brand that I know of is Westbrae Natural 50%-Less-Sodium Soy Sauce, which contains 430 milligrams of sodium per tablespoon. Look for this product in natural food stores throughout the country. Always be sure to buy a soy sauce or tamari sauce that contains no preservatives.

64 ▪ **Or try Bragg's Liquid Amino Acids,** a soy sauce alternative that contains 630 milligrams of sodium per table-spoon. The sodium in this condiment is a healthy source because the sodium is derived entirely from specially formulated soy protein. Unlike soy sauce, the product is not brewed or fermented, and it does not have any MSG, alcohol, chemicals, preservatives, or added salt. Therefore, Bragg's Liquid Amino Acids is particularly well tolerated even by many individuals who are afflicted with chemical sensitivities. It is worth making a trip to your local health food store to find.

65 ▪ **Miso** is a fermented soy paste that has the consistency of peanut butter and is used primarily in Japanese and macrobiotic cooking as a flavorful condiment, soup starter, or spread. There are twenty-nine varieties of miso, and each one has a different flavor and degree of saltiness. Light-colored varieties such as chickpea miso usually are sweet and lower in salt, whereas darker varieties like hatcho miso have a meatier taste and higher salt content. No matter which type you choose, look for unpasteurized miso (sold in round plastic tubs in the refrigerator case in natural food stores) because it contains a wealth of beneficial natural enzymes produced by lactobacillus, yeasts, and other microorganisms that stimulate digestion. Take care not to boil miso, however, because boiling kills the live bacteria in it and diminishes its rich aroma. Miso is a potent seasoning and it does contain natural MSG, so it is best used in small amounts.

66 ▪ Cheese should be used more as a condiment in place of salt than as one of your dietary mainstays. That is because cheese is a good source of valuable calcium, but it also can be a significant source of undesirable salt and saturated fat. To lower your salt intake, always choose natural cheese instead of higher-salt processed cheese products. While even natural cheese is salty, it is still far lower in salt than most processed foods, and it is more nutritious.

▪ BONUS TIP: *Although few people realize it because dairy products do not taste salty, dairy products are good sources of bioavailable sodium. Some sodium-sensitive individuals may need to limit their consumption of dairy products, especially their intake of salt-rich cheese and buttermilk. Individuals who have low-sodium levels, however, may want to increase their intake of these foods.*

67 ▪ Higher-sodium vegetables, such as celery, carrots, beets, parsley, chard, kale, and spinach, can be used to impart naturally salty flavors in cooked foods. If you have a low-sodium blood level, emphasize these foods in your diet to increase your sodium intake.

68 ▪ Salt-free herbal seasonings are the safest and best alternatives to salt for sodium-sensitive individuals. Made from flavorful herbs that contain more minerals like potassium and magnesium than sodium, salt-free seasonings come in a multitude of tasty varieties and are a real boon for anyone trying to reduce his or her sodium intake. When choosing a seasoning, be sure to buy one that does not contain MSG in any of its various forms. (See tip 90 for more information.) One good brand to try is The Spice Hunter, which does not add MSG to any of its sixty different varieties of salt-free blends.

69 ▪ Try making your own herbal seasoning. This way, you can be sure to avoid both salt and MSG, and you can experiment with blends that suit your tastes. Here are a few suggestions of herbal combinations that make excellent, piquant salt substitutes:

> Equal parts ground cayenne and dried mint leaves
> Equal parts dried marjoram, dried sage, ground cumin seed, and ground celery seed
> Four parts onion powder, two parts paprika, two parts garlic powder, and three parts cayenne pepper
> Two parts peppercorns, one part allspice berry, and one part mustard seed, ground in a pepper mill as needed

Remember that freshly ground or crushed herbs and spices have the strongest flavor and aroma.

70 ▪ Salt substitutes made with potassium chloride may sound like a good idea, but they should be avoided. Although these products do supply additional potassium in the diet, the potassium they supply is unnatural, and the body does not utilize it well. They also contain the same undesirable chemical additives found in table salt. In large amounts, potassium salts can cause nausea, vomiting, diarrhea, and ulcers, and they sometimes distort the flavor in foods and leave a bitter taste. The best way to get salt out of your diet is to use the tips in this book, not to turn to artificial replacements.

71 ▪ Determine which kind of salt or salt alternative is best for you. One person may feel best using miso (see tip 65) or reduced-sodium tamari (see tip 63) while another may tolerate Real Salt better. Since our individual body chemistries are so different, we need to choose the sodium sources we feel best eating on an individual basis as well.

SUPERMARKET SAVVY

72 ▪ **Shop for groceries mainly in the outer aisles of your supermarket** —the produce, meat, dairy, and bulk food sections. These sections carry mostly natural foods that have little or no salt added. A grocery store's inner aisles, however, are home to foods that are loaded with salt and sodium preservatives so they can sit on the shelf for long periods of time without spoiling. If you limit the groceries you pick up from the inner aisles and buy mostly natural foods from the outer aisles, you will automatically reduce your sodium consumption dramatically.

73 ▪ **Take trips to your local natural food store** to seek out better forms of salt and salted foods. You should be able to find a wider selection of unsalted foods there as well as unrefined sea salt or Real Salt. Contrary to the beliefs of some of my clients, however, not all foods carried in health food stores are low in sodium. Though the foods carried there are usually superior alternatives to the salted foods normally found in regular supermarkets, always check the nutrition labels to be sure.

74 ▪ **Become a label reader.** No matter where you buy your food, you have to pay attention to what's in it. Don't forget that the overwhelming majority of the salt Americans consume is "hidden" in processed foods. This means that you have to be skeptical about every food you're thinking of buying. If you do nothing else to lower your sodium intake, read those labels and don't let the "hidden" sodium sneak past you.

75 ▪ **Label Reading Lesson No. 1:** Read the number of sodium milligrams listed on the Nutrition Facts label of the food you're considering buying. Although sodium requirements differ for each individual, use this as a rule of thumb: focus on buying low-sodium foods—foods that have *140 milligrams or less* of sodium per serving—and make these your staples. (If you need additional sodium in your diet, add extra natural salt at the table.)

76 ▪ If it helps you to understand milligrams of sodium in terms of teaspoons of salt, remember that there are 2,000 milligrams of sodium in just one teaspoon of salt. That amount is more than sufficient for most of us in a single day. With this in mind, understand that a TV dinner that has 1,500 milligrams of sodium supplies *three-quarters* of that amount.

77 ▪ Label Reading Lesson No. 2: Check the "% Daily Value" of sodium the product provides. Never buy foods that contain *more than 16 percent* of the Daily Value of sodium. If you'd like to emphasize *Two Salt Shaker* foods in your diet, buy foods that contain *less than 10 percent* of the Daily Value, or if you'd like to eat predominantly *One Salt Shaker* foods (something most of us should do), choose foods that contain *less than 6 percent* of the Daily Value. If you buy and eat foods with more than 16 percent, be especially conscious of the sodium levels of the other foods you eat that day.

78 ▪ Label Reading Lesson No. 3: Peruse the ingredient list and look for sodium in all its various forms. It can be listed as any of the following: baking powder, baking soda, disodium phosphate, monosodium glutamate (MSG), salt, sea salt, sodium alginate, sodium aluminum sulfate, sodium ascorbate, sodium benzoate, sodium bisulfite, sodium carboxymethyl cellulose, sodium caseinate, sodium erythorbate, sodium hexametaphosphate, sodium hydroxide, sodium nitrite, sodium nitrate, sodium pectinate, sodium propionate, sodium pyrophosphate, sodium saccharin, and sodium sulfite.

▪ BONUS TIP: *Not only are these ingredients unhealthy sources of sodium that the body can't easily use, but many of them also are chemicals that have been proven to jeopardize our health. Avoiding unnecessary chemicals in our diet is just as important as avoiding refined salt.*

79 ▪ **Label Reading Lesson No. 3 (Short Version):** A quick way to discern sodium on the label is simply to look for the words *salt* or *sodium* in any form or for the chemical symbols Na or NaCl.

▪ **BONUS TIP:** *While you're reading the label for sodium content, pay attention to the other ingredients in the food as well. If you have no idea what some ingredients are, the chances are good that your body has no idea what to do with the ingredients either. Avoid the fake foods and instead buy nutritious products that contain identifiable whole foods the body knows how to use.*

80 ▪ **Label Reading Lesson No. 4:** If you have high blood pressure, you should compare the milligrams of potassium a food has in relation to its sodium milligrams and choose foods that have much more potassium than sodium. Unfortunately, it's not always easy to choose high-potassium foods because most manufacturers do not voluntarily provide information about potassium content on their labels. However, some companies such as Arrowhead Mills do. This is a true service to those customers trying to reduce high blood pressure by increasing potassium intake at the same time they reduce sodium.

81 ▪ **Understand the meaning of "sodium-free"** and other recently regulated terms under the FDA's new food-labeling rules. "Sodium-free" means that the food contains negligible sodium—*less than 5 milligrams per serving.*

82 ▪ **"Very-low-sodium"** is a nutrient claim given to foods that have *35 milligrams or less* of sodium per serving. Both "very-low-sodium" and "sodium-free" are good terms to look for when your diet requires strict control of your sodium intake.

83 ▪ **"Low-sodium"** refers to foods that contain *140 milligrams or less* of sodium per serving. (All tips given the *One Salt*

Shaker designation in this book meet this definition.) If you don't know how to start reducing your sodium consumption, just begin by buying "low-sodium" foods. You can eat these foods frequently throughout the day without exceeding the FDA's guidelines for sodium.

84 ▪ "Light" can mean several things under the FDA's new labeling regulations. When referring to sodium, "light" can signify low-calorie, low-fat foods whose sodium content has been reduced by at least *50 percent*. If the sodium level of a food has been reduced by one-half but the food is not low in calories and fat, the label must be specific by saying "light in sodium."

85 ▪ "Less" or "fewer" are terms that can help you choose foods that have been altered to contain a certain percentage less sodium than a comparable food that is normally salted. This means that a soup may contain "20 percent less sodium" than the original soup, for example.

86 ▪ A "reduced-sodium" product contains *at least 25 percent less sodium* than the regular product. This applies only to products that were not low in sodium to begin with. (If you're confused by this regulation, don't feel badly. This rule is tricky and hard to understand even for seasoned nutritionists.) To keep it simple, remember to choose "low-sodium" foods over "reduced-sodium" foods whenever possible.

87 ▪ "Unsalted," "without-added-salt," and "no-salt-added" mean that no salt was added during processing of the product and indicate that the food is usually processed with salt. (In other words, these terms would not apply to sorbets, candies, or anything that doesn't normally contain salt.)

88 ▪ Also look for foods that are labeled "good sources" or "high sources" of potassium, magnesium, and calcium. These three minerals are known to counteract some of the effects of a high-sodium diet and can be protective against—

and even therapeutic for—both hypertension and heart disease. (To be labeled a "good source" of one of these nutrients, one food serving must supply *between 10 and 19 percent* of the Daily Value for that nutrient. If a food supplies *20 percent or more* of the Daily Value for a particular nutrient, it legally can be called a "high source" of that nutrient.)

89 ▪ No matter how much food labels help you select low-salt foods, understand that the best foods are the natural ones that have no labels to tout their many benefits. For example, a potato found in your supermarket produce section probably won't have a label, but if it did, the label would claim "very-low-sodium" and "high in potassium" (not to mention "cholesterol-free" and "99% fat-free"). These all are accurate claims about the potato, but because fresh produce requires no labeling, many of us don't know these facts.

90 ▪ To avoid buying groceries that contain MSG (monosodium glutamate), become a supersavvy food consumer by steering clear of MSG's other aliases. According to Russell L. Blaylock in *Excitotoxins: The Taste That Kills* (Health Press, 1994), ingredients that always contain MSG include: hydrolyzed vegetable protein, hydrolyzed protein, hydrolyzed plant protein, plant protein extract, sodium caseinate, calcium caseinate, yeast extract, textured protein, autolyzed yeast, and hydrolyzed oat flour. Other additives that frequently contain MSG include: malt extract, malt flavoring, bouillon, broth, stock, and natural flavorings.

91 ▪ Become familiar with groups of foods that are *very likely* to contain MSG. According to *In Bad Taste: The MSG Syndrome* by George R. Schwartz, M.D., these include: potato chips and prepared snacks; canned soups and dry soup mixes; canned meats; boxed dinners; prepared meals; frozen dinner entrées; salad dressings; cured meats; lunch meats; and international foods. According to Dr. Schwartz, MSG can be disguised under the following names, particularly in international foods: Ajinomoto; Zest; Vetsin; gourmet powder; Subu; Chinese seasoning; Glutavene; Glutacyl; RL-50; Mei-jing; and Wei-jing.

92 ▪ **If you're severely allergic to MSG,** call or write the manufacturer directly to find out if a food product is free of MSG.

93 ▪ **Or find reputable products in health food stores** that are labeled "no MSG" or "no MSG added."

94 ▪ **If your local grocery store doesn't carry products that meet your needs,** speak up about it! If enough consumers tell supermarket managers how unhappy they are with the high-sodium foods currently being offered, I can promise you that a more healthful variety of foods will appear. In the meantime, it's up to you to ask for the kinds of foods you want. Request—maybe even politely insist—that the store begin to carry or at least take a special order for some of the low-sodium and MSG-free foods mentioned in this book.

95 ▪ **Never go grocery shopping when you're hungry.** This is just as basic a rule for those who consume too much salt as it is for those who consume too much sugar. If your stomach is empty as you browse the aisles, your weak adrenals will beckon you to grab high-salt and high-sugar foods that give your adrenals a quick—but artificial and temporary—lift. To avoid the trap of bringing home more salty foods than you bargained for, eat sensibly before you go shopping so you can buy sensibly when you're there.

▪ ▪ ▪

LOWER-SODIUM COOKING SUBSTITUTIONS

96 ▪ **Don't concern yourself with the sodium content of natural foods** in recipes. If the food is fresh and unprocessed, the sodium content really is too small to worry about.

97 ▪ **Instead, focus your attention on avoiding salt-laden processed foods;** this is the key to cutting sodium in recipes. When a recipe calls for any of the following ingredients, substitute the corresponding lower-sodium alternative:

98 ▪ **Table salt:** herbs or salt-free herbal blends of your choice. (Salt-free all-purpose blends are the most common substitution.)

99 ▪ **Celery salt:** celery flakes.

100 ▪ **Garlic salt:** garlic powder.

101 ▪ **Onion salt:** onion powder.

102 ▪ **Tomato paste:** salt-free tomato paste.

103 ▪ **Tomato sauce:** a tomato sauce with no salt added— or make your own by blending two cans of water with one can of salt-free tomato paste.

104 ▪ **Canned tomato juice or vegetable juice cocktail:** low-sodium tomato juice or low-sodium vegetable juice cocktail. If the taste of the low-sodium version is too bland for you, make it zestier by pouring the juice into a glass bottle and adding one whole green onion and several pieces of diced celery. Let it sit for a few hours, strain it, then taste the flavorful transformation.

105 ▪ **Canned tomatoes:** canned tomatoes that are salt-free or have no salt added.

106 ▪ **Soy sauce or tamari sauce:** reduced-sodium soy sauce, reduced-sodium tamari sauce, or Bragg's Liquid Amino Acids. (See tips 63 and 64.)

107 ▪ **Canned soup or broth:** homemade or low-sodium canned soup or broth. (See chapter 4 for more information.)

108 ▪ **Cooking wine or cooking sherry:** table wine or drinking wine or sherry. Most people don't realize it, but cooking wine has added salt, an addition that is totally unnecessary because wine that is cooked into foods is tremendously flavorful all by itself. It's interesting to note that the term "cooking wine" goes back in history to a time when wine set aside for use in food was salted to prevent the cook from drinking it.

109 ▪ **Butter or margarine:** unsalted butter.

▪ BONUS TIP: *Always choose butter in place of margarine, no matter what you may have heard to the contrary. Yes, butter does contain saturated fat, but our bodies can handle saturated fats in small amounts. Far more damaging to the human body than saturated fats are* trans-fats—*hydrogenated and partially hydrogenated oils found in products like margarine. Our bodies were not designed to handle these unnatural fats, which are now known to lower "good" HDL cholesterol levels, raise "bad" LDL levels, and increase the risk of heart disease. The French seem to prove this point: they eat butter and other forms of saturated fats but no trans-fats (and also less sugar). Consequently, they have a much lower rate of heart disease than Americans do. Excessive use of butter isn't good either, but using a little bit of butter is far better than using any margarine.*

110 ▪ **Cheese and cottage cheese:** reduced-sodium cheese and low-sodium, dry-curd cottage cheese. (If cheese is eaten moderately, this substitution is not necessary for most individuals. It is helpful, however, for individuals who need to greatly reduce their overall sodium intake or for those who want to reduce the salt content in a particular meal that contains these ingredients.)

▪ ▪ ▪

THE FINE ART OF MODERATION

111 ▪ Do not restrict yourself so much that you end up bingeing on salt. Human nature is such that we always seem to yearn for things we aren't supposed to have. My philosophy is to go ahead and satisfy your taste for salt, but do so intelligently and moderately. In the long run, this strategy is more effective and *better for you* than total abstinence, which can cause health problems.

112 ▪ Substitute healthy salty snacks for salty junk food. (This book will show you how.) Then eat these treats slowly, so your taste buds can savor every salty morsel.

113 ▪ Split salty foods with others and replace the food you're missing with more fresh foods. In other words, instead of devouring half of a high-salt pizza, have a slice or two along with a big, fresh, low-sodium salad.

114 ▪ Allow yourself indulgences during special occasions and vacations as long as you resume a healthier, lower-sodium diet once your regular routine begins again.

115 ▪ Do the best you can to avoid foods that contain unnecessary sodium, but don't berate yourself if you aren't always perfect. If you ate more salt today than you would have liked, accept it and just vow to eat better tomorrow.

116 ▪ Remember that while avoiding table salt is important for good health, it is not the *only* thing that promotes health. By all means, try to get the salt out of your diet, but not to the point of obsession. Be sure to keep salt reduction in perspective with other factors that contribute to a healthy quality of life: avoidance of unhealthy trans-fats, refined sugar, refined carbohydrates, and chemicals; regular exercise; a positive self-image; and meaningful work and personal relationships.

CHAPTER 2

Get the Salt Out
of Your Water

Water. The only liquid that by itself is a nutrient to humans. This indispensable fluid comprises almost two-thirds of the body's mass and hydrates every living cell. Water also transports nutrients into vital organs like the heart and carries away waste material. Water is so important to human health that we can go a week or more without food but only three to five days without water.

Unfortunately, most of us have taken water for granted. For decades, we've used water carelessly for our own convenience, without realizing that we've been contaminating one of the most important substances that nourishes us. Our use of water softeners is a perfect example of our neglectful use of water. By removing beneficial calcium and magnesium from hard water and replacing these minerals with excessive amounts of sodium, we have altered water so that it may help soaps lather up better, but we also have altered it so that it is a health hazard for ourselves and an environmental hazard for our planet.

Humans can't survive long on salty water. Shipwrecked sailors throughout history are a testament to this fact: many have died trying to quench their thirst with salty seawater. If you remember that drinking seawater is harmful and eventually lethal to humans, then it's easy to understand why drinking salt-contaminated water also is dangerous.

Drinking is not the only way we absorb salt from water. Our digestive systems also absorb salt from foods that are cooked in salted water, and our skin topically picks up salt from water we bathe in. My experience counseling clients for more than twenty years has shown that drinking water, cooking water, and bathing water often are overlooked keys to excess sodium levels.

The tips in this chapter provide rarely covered information about water. They will give you the incentive and the know-how to get the salt out of your water as well as your food.

DRINKING WATER

117 ▪ Never drink salt-softened water in place of hard water. Many studies have shown that people who drink hard water have lower rates of heart disease than people who drink softened water. This is because hard water is rich in hard-to-find minerals that are protective against heart disease. Hard water's mineral content is so impressive that it can rival that found in mineral-rich foods. One liter of hard drinking water, for example, can provide up to 375 milligrams of calcium. By comparison, one of the best sources of calcium, a three-ounce can of sardines, contains 372 milligrams, but it also contains undesirably high amounts of sodium.

118 ▪ If you have high blood pressure or high-sodium levels, find out the sodium content of your tap water through your local water department or health department. Your drinking water sometimes can sabotage a healthful, low-sodium diet by contributing as much as 3,750 milligrams of sodium in ten eight-ounce glasses! People who live in snowy areas where road salt is used or those who live in coastal communities frequently have saltier water than individuals who live in other areas. If you are on a sodium-restricted diet and your tap water's sodium content is more than 80 parts per million, the American Heart Association recommends that you switch to sodium-free bottled water. *One Salt Shaker.*

119 ▪ Know that all bottled waters are not low in sodium. Some, in fact, contain more than 1,000 milligrams of sodium in every liter! That's more than 250 milligrams per cup! The following are particularly high-sodium brands you should avoid: Kaiser Friedrich Quelle, Laoshan, Saint Yorre, San Narciso, Uberkinger, Vichy Catalan, Vichy Celestins, and Vichy Springs.

120 ▪ Drink bottled water that is low in sodium and that contains more heart-healthy calcium and magnesium than sodium. Brands of bottled water that meet these criteria are: Arrowhead, Evian, Golden Eagle, La Croix, Vichy Novella, and Vittel Grande. *One Salt Shaker.*

121 ▪ Read the labels on other brands of bottled water and look for water that is low in sodium (containing 140 milligrams of sodium or less per serving), very low in sodium (containing 35 milligrams of sodium or less per serving), or sodium-free. Although it's a good idea to drink a bottled water rich in both calcium and magnesium when it's available, your second-best choice is any water that is low in sodium, such as popular brands like Calistoga, Crystal Geyser, Perrier, and Poland Spring. *One Salt Shaker.*

122 ▪ Try to drink at least eight glasses of low-sodium water each day. Despite what many people believe, drinking more water does not cause bloating and water retention. Quite the contrary; it is a simple way of flushing unnecesary salt out of the body and of reducing bloating. Just be sure the water you drink is low in sodium. *One Salt Shaker.*

▪ BONUS TIP: *In addition to drinking low-sodium water, it's also tremendously important to drink water that is free of chlorine, chemicals, lead, rust, and pathogenic bacteria and parasites. A high-quality water filter takes out impurities like these and gives you clean water that will support optimal health. To receive more information about the Doulton of England water filters that I recommend to my clients, call Uni Key Health Systems, which is listed in the Resources section.*

123 ▪ **Always opt for seltzer instead of club soda.** Both are made from tap water that is filtered and carbonated, but club soda is higher in sodium because it has mineral salts added to it. Common ingredients added to club soda include sodium bicarbonate (baking soda), sodium chloride (salt), and sometimes disodium phosphate. Remember that the lower-sodium choice always is seltzer.

COOKING WATER

124 ▪ **Refrain from adding salt to cooking water when you prepare pasta, cereals, and grains.** Even though package directions usually call for it, adding salt simply is not necessary and can contribute hundreds of unwanted sodium milligrams per dish. Many people think the addition of salt lowers the boiling point of water, but in fact it has no effect on the water's boiling temperature in the amounts normally added. *One Salt Shaker.*

125 ▪ **When cooking grains and spaghetti, try adding a bay leaf to cooking water in place of salt.** It is such a nice substitute that nutritionist Judith Benn Hurley calls bay leaf "the sodium slasher." *One Salt Shaker.*

126 ▪ Or add a few drops of fresh lemon juice or a pinch of herbs to the cooking water. This is a creative way to eliminate the salt and give pasta and grains a more refreshing flavor. *One Salt Shaker.*

127 ▪ If you think cooking food in salted water couldn't possibly affect your health, consider this: in the 1970s, two tribes in the Solomon Islands were found to have very similar lifestyles and diets, but one of the tribes, the Lau, cooked their vegetables in seawater, and the other tribe, the Aita, did not. The Aita consumed about 500 milligrams of sodium each day and did not have one case of hypertension among them. The Lau, on the other hand, consumed 3,000 to 4,500 extra sodium milligrams each day from its practice of cooking with salty seawater, and 10 percent of the population suffered from high blood pressure.

BATHING WATER

128 ▪ Switch to bathing in magnetically conditioned water instead of salt-softened water. Many people prefer to bathe with salt-softened water because it doesn't leave mineral deposits and because soaps work better in it. Unfortunately though, the cleansing benefits of softened water come with an undesirable trade-off: softened water increases the risk of heart disease and may also contribute to goiters and gallbladder disease. Even worse, fatal heart attacks and strokes are much more common in areas where softened water is used. Instead of using a water softener, which replaces valuable calcium and magnesium with sodium, use a magnetic water conditioner, which changes the orientation of water's mineral ions. Hard water treated in this way will "behave" as if it was softened (in other words, as if the mineral content was lowered). This gives you the best of both worlds: all of the beneficial minerals present in hard water along with many of the cleansing benefits salt-softened water provides. To purchase or learn more about magnetic water conditioners, see the GMX listing in the Resources section.

129 ▪ Keep this in mind: getting the salt out of your bathing water is good for the environment. A research project conducted at Wayne State University found that salt from water softeners is a potential source of groundwater contamination. This is alarming because a large portion of our drinking water comes from groundwater sources. The average household with a water softener uses an eighty-pound bag of salt to treat its water each month. Ultimately, this results in close to a thousand pounds of salt being dumped into the ground each year—by a single family! When you use a water conditioner that does not use salt, you not only improve your health, but you do your part to protect the health of the planet as well.

130 ▪ Use the skin's efficient ability to absorb minerals to your advantage, not to your disadvantage. Nutritionist Martin Fox has noted that an adult who takes a fifteen-minute bath typically absorbs almost twice as much water—and the substances dissolved in it—as he or she receives from a day's supply of drinking water. This means that you can add magnesium-rich Epsom salts to bathwater to increase your absorption of heart-healthy magnesium, but you must avoid using salt-softened water, particularly if you bathe frequently.

CHAPTER 3

Get the Salt Out of Breakfast

Breakfast is the most important meal of the day, but it frequently is an afterthought to many individuals. In today's fast-paced world, Americans often start their day with instant foods, which almost always means salty foods. Whether they eat a sausage biscuit from a drive-through or hurriedly eat a bowl of ready-to-eat cereal, they usually consume excessive levels of unhealthy sodium and refined salt whenever they choose convenience for breakfast over nutrition.

Few of us realize it, but the nutrition we receive during breakfast can have a huge impact on how we feel and even on what we eat the rest of the day. Judging from my clients' cases, too many people lag in energy because they eat the wrong foods for breakfast. They mistakenly believe all protein and fats are bad and all carbohydrates are healthy, so they avoid quality foods—like eggs—that could keep them going for hours. Instead, they load up on nutrient-poor processed carbohydrates such as white bread, croissants, English muffins, and bagels. These foods are so tasteless on their own (having been stripped of the very parts that give them the most flavor) that they often have to be made with salt or topped with a salty spread like butter to be palatable. Even worse, processed carbohydrates like these lose important minerals like magnesium and potassium that would otherwise offset the effects of added sodium. In addition, eating refined carbohydrates ultimately can cause people to eat more salt: when individuals eat these foods at the beginning of the day, they often crave and may even binge on salty junk food and sugary snacks just a few hours after breakfast to get a quick, but short-lived, jolt of the energy they lack. (Both salt and sugar *temporarily* stimulate the energy-producing adrenal glands.)

An important key to reducing salt intake is to eat a healthy breakfast that is not only low in sodium but also nutritious enough to prevent bingeing on salt later in the day. Eating a healthy breakfast does not need to be complicated or time-consuming. It simply requires switching to whole-grain carbohydrates and balancing them with small amounts of quality protein and fats for longer-term energy.

The tips in this chapter will help you do that. You'll learn how to get the salt out of breakfast while you keep convenience, flavor, and long-lasting nutrition in.

BREADS AND SPREADS

131 ▪ Choose whole grain bread that is low in sodium. Commercial yeasted bread always has salt added to it to prevent the bread from rising too much and developing a strong yeasty taste. To prevent consuming more sodium than you bargained for, try to find bread that contains *less than 140 milligrams of sodium per slice* and that is made with sea salt instead of regular table salt. *One Salt Shaker.*

132 ▪ **Never use self-rising flour** if you bake bread or biscuits at home. Self-rising flour has salt and leavening agents already added to it, a process that creates an outrageously high-sodium product. (Gold Medal Self-Rising Flour, for example, contains 1,520 milligrams of sodium per cup and Aunt Jemima's Self-Rising Flour actually contains 3,176 milligrams of sodium per cup!) The unhealthy sodium content of self-rising flour obviously is dangerous. Avoid using this product at all costs.

133 ▪ **If you make your own bread,** you can make it without salt as long as you follow these instructions: when the dough is rising in the bowl, occasionally punch it lightly with two fingers to prevent excessive rising. When the indentation of your fingers no longer bounces back, it's time to shape the dough and bake it. *One Salt Shaker.*

134 ▪ **Why eat whole grain bread?** Because it is rich in nutrients that help control the effects of overconsumption of sodium. It also has great flavor, texture, and chewiness and is delicious on its own—certainly better butterless than white or mostly white bread.

135 ▪ **Try whole grain sourdough bread for a great change of pace.** Since sourdough bread is not made with yeast, it has no sugar and also is low in salt and sodium. Instead of yeast, sourdough bread is naturally leavened with fermenting agents that break down the flour's cellulose structure, neutralize its mineral-inhibiting phytic acid, and release more nutrients into the dough. The result is a bread that supplies more minerals that are easier for your body to absorb. French Meadow Bakery makes a particularly nice line of sourdough breads that are low in sodium (even though they don't taste low in sodium). It is also one of the few companies I know of that goes to the extra trouble and expense to use healthy, unrefined sea salt in its products instead of table salt. Look for this healthful brand in natural food stores throughout the country. *One to Two Salt Shakers* (depending on the variety).

136 ▪ **A dab of sweet butter is a satisfying way to top toast, even when you use unsalted butter.** For additional sweetness as a spread, top butter with a light sprinkling of cinnamon. (If you're concerned about eating butter, see the Bonus Tip to tip 109 for additional information.) *One Salt Shaker.*

137 ▪ **Is rye toast with unsalted butter too bland for you?** Try dressing it up German-style with savory Caraway Butter. This idea and recipe was developed by nutritionist Melissa Diane Smith. *One Salt Shaker.*

▪ **CARAWAY BUTTER** ▪

$1/3$ cup unsalted whipped butter
1 teaspoon caraway seeds

Crush the caraway seeds between 2 spoons for the freshest flavor. Put the unsalted whipped butter in a coffee cup or small bowl and let it soften slightly at room temperature. Then cream the butter and the crushed caraway seeds together with a spoon until well mixed. Spread on toasted rye or sourdough rye bread by the teaspoonful or store in a covered container in the refrigerator for a few days. *Makes about $1/4$ cup.*

▪ BONUS TIP: *Add a few teaspoons of unrefined flaxseed oil or walnut oil (which you can find in health food stores) to the recipe above to increase your intake of beneficial Omega 3 essential fatty acids (EFAs). Often called the "good fats," Omega 3 EFAs are necessary for proper functioning of the heart and can lower high blood pressure.*

138 ▪ **Another great spread to top toast** is unsalted peanut butter or any other unsalted nut or seed butter of your choice. Nut and seed butters are rich sources of heart-healthy magnesium and potassium, which are in short supply in the typical American diet. In addition, whole grain bread spread with unsalted nut butter is one of the ultimate fast foods: it's quick to make, low in sodium, and packed with nutrition. Look for nut butters labeled "unsalted" or "no salt added" by companies like Arrowhead Mills, Marantha Natural Foods, or Roaster-Fresh by Kettle Foods in natural food stores. These brands do not contain the unhealthy hydrogenated oils and sugar found in most commercial nut butters. *One Salt Shaker.*

139 ▪ Skip the bagels and opt for a slice or two of low-sodium, whole grain bread. Bagels are surprisingly high in salt: one three-ounce plain Sara Lee bagel, for example, contains 580 milligrams of sodium. If you want to treat yourself to a small amount of cream cheese (which has only 84 milligrams of sodium per ounce), spread it on low-sodium bread instead of a bagel. *One to Two Salt Shakers.*

140 ▪ Yogurt cheese is a delightful spread for bread as well. To make it, simply line a colander with cheesecloth and place a bowl underneath. Pour 2 cups of plain nonfat yogurt (by itself or mixed with a dash of nutmeg, cinnamon, cardamom, or vanilla extract) on top of the cheesecloth. Put everything in the refrigerator, cover the yogurt, and let it drain overnight. What remains is a delicious cheese that is low in sodium and a good source of calcium and potassium. *One Salt Shaker.*

BREAKFAST GOODIES

141 ▪ A whole grain, low-sugar muffin is better for your blood pressure than a couple of slices of whole grain toast. Even if both the muffin and the toast have the same sodium content, the sodium contained in most baked goods (sodium bicarbonate) is less "dangerous" to the body than the sodium chloride (or salt) found in bread. In both human and animal studies, researchers have found a greater increase in blood pressure among those receiving sodium chloride than among those receiving other forms of sodium like sodium bicarbonate. To raise blood pressure, you need both the sodium ion and the chloride ion, as in table salt. Sodium chloride raises blood volume, increases urinary excretion of calcium, and induces increases in the systolic and diastolic blood pressure—all of which can double or triple the risk of heart attack and stroke. For all of these reasons, a muffin is better for you than toast *as long as the muffin you eat is low in sugar.* (Too much sugar has been found to contribute to both high blood pressure and heart disease, just like too much salt.)

▪ BONUS TIP: *If you need help reducing the sugar you consume in muffins and other foods, you may want to read my book* Get the Sugar Out, *which provides 501 tips on how to do exactly that.*

142 ▪ **Use mashed sweet vegetables and fruits** —like mashed sweet potato, winter squash, or applesauce—when you use sodium-rich leavening agents like baking soda and regular baking powder in baked goods. Mashed vegetables and fruits provide potassium, which counteracts the sodium content of the leavening agents. They also make muffins naturally sweet and moist. The following muffin recipe, from *Back to Health* by Dennis W. Remington, M.D., and Barbara W. Higa, R.D., uses high-potassium mashed banana in this way. *Two Salt Shakers.*

▪ ▪ ▪

▪ WHEAT-FREE BANANA MUFFINS ▪

1 cup rolled oats
1¹/₂ cups oat bran
¹/₂ cup chopped nuts
¹/₄ teaspoon salt
1 tablespoon baking powder
1 banana, mashed
2 eggs, lightly beaten
3 tablespoons cold-pressed oil
2 tablespoons honey
³/₄ cup milk

Combine the dry ingredients [oats, oat bran, nuts, salt, and baking powder] in a bowl. Mix together the mashed banana, eggs, oil, honey, and milk. Add this mixture to the dry ingredients and combine only until moistened. Fill 12 oiled or paper-lined muffin cups ²/₃ full. Bake at 400 degrees for about 20 minutes. *Makes 12 muffins.*

143 ▪ Stay away from foods like toaster pastries, fruit turnovers, and danish pastries. Although you may know that these foods are high in nutrient-depleting refined carbohydrates and sugar, you may not realize that they also are surprisingly high sources of sodium.

144 ▪ Make your own pancakes and waffles. If you make homemade breakfast goodies instead of relying on high-sodium, highly processed mixes, you'll eat much less sodium. According to *The Sodium Counter* (Pocket Books, 1993), three pancakes made from Aunt Jemima Whole Wheat Pancake and Waffle Mix contain a whopping 950 milligrams! The same number of pancakes made from scratch at home usually contains only a few hundred.

145 ▪ To reduce the sodium content of baked goods even

further, use Featherweight or Cellu low-sodium baking powder in place of regular baking powder. The pancakes that follow are simple to make and nutritious but contain only 14 milligrams of sodium each. This recipe comes from *Salt: The Brand Name Guide to Sodium Content* by the Center for Science in the Public Interest (CSPI). *One Salt Shaker.*

▪ WHOLE-WHEAT PANCAKES ▪

$1^1/_2$ cups whole wheat flour
$1^1/_2$ teaspoons low-sodium baking powder
2 teaspoons honey or frozen apple juice concentrate
1 egg, beaten
$1^1/_2$ cups skim milk
2 tablespoons unsalted butter, melted, or oil

In a bowl, mix together the flour and baking powder. In a separate bowl, mix together the honey or apple juice concentrate, egg, and milk. Add the wet ingredients to the flour mixture and stir until the batter is lump-free. Place a nonstick griddle over medium-high heat, and when it is hot, grease it with a small amount of the melted butter or oil. Ladle out a small amount of the batter and carefully pour it onto the griddle to form a pancake. If it is under 3 inches wide, add more batter; if it is larger, ladle on less batter for the other pancakes. When the batter bubbles lightly and the edges seem firm, flip the pancakes over with a spatula. Cook for another minute or so. Continue cooking the pancakes, greasing the griddle if it gets too dry and adjusting the heat if the pancakes seem to be cooking too quickly. *Makes sixteen to eighteen 3-inch-wide pancakes.*

146 ▪ **You also can skip baking powder and baking soda altogether** and use the natural leavening action of eggs to help foods like waffles rise. That's exactly what Dr. Remington and

Barbara Higa did in this recipe from their book, *Back to Health.*
One Salt Shaker.

▪ ANNETTE'S OATMEAL WAFFLES ▪

2 eggs
4 tablespoons cold-pressed oil
3 cups warm milk
3 cups rolled oats
Dash of salt

Whip the eggs and oil together in a blender until thoroughly
mixed. Add warm milk, rolled oats, and salt and process in the
blender until smooth. Place in a preheated, lightly oiled waffle
iron and bake approximately 10 minutes. *Makes six 7-inch waffles.*

**147 ▪ If toasting a frozen waffle is more your style than
making waffles from scratch,** have on hand frozen waffles by
Van's International, which you can find in health food stores.
Van's waffles are made with wholesome ingredients and are
much lower in sodium than commercial brands. Two Van's
Multi-Grain Toaster Waffles contain only 135 milligrams of
sodium compared to 400 milligrams of sodium in two Kellogg's
Nutri-Grain Multi-Grain Eggo's. *One to Two Salt Shakers*
(depending on the variety).

**148 ▪ Reach for very-low-sodium or sodium-free natural
sweeteners to top pancakes** instead of artificially flavored pancake and waffle toppings. I never have been able to understand
why salt is in pancake syrups anyway, but it often is —along
with other sodium-containing additives. Remember, when in
doubt, opt for the more natural choice. For pancake toppings,
that means a small amount of 100 percent pure maple syrup or
honey. *One Salt Shaker.*

149 ▪ **Better yet, top pancakes with unsweetened apple-sauce or fresh fruit.** These sweet toppings are much lower in sugar than maple syrup or honey, and they are rich in potassium and virtually sodium-free. *One Salt Shaker.*

BREAKFAST ENTRÉES

---

150 ▪ **Make eggs without salt** or at least don't add salt until after the eggs have cooked. Salt makes egg whites tough and will cause them to break up in poaching water. It also causes scrambled eggs to turn out drier and less fluffy than if they are made without salt.

151 ▪ **Enjoy a poached or hard-boiled egg with a dash of salt-free herbal seasoning** like The Spice Hunter All-Purpose Blend. (See tip 68.) If you're concerned that eating the egg yolk is unhealthy, don't be: it is one of the richest sources of pantothenic acid, a vitamin that promotes healthy adrenal function and, therefore, healthy sodium metabolism. In addition, though it contains some cholesterol, the yolk is high in lecithin, which is a cholesterol-lowering agent. *One Salt Shaker.*

▪ BONUS TIP: *If you have bitten into the common misconception that eggs should be avoided because of their cholesterol content, you should know that only one study has ever found eggs to be dangerous. That study was sponsored by the Cereal Institute, which had good reason to interest Americans in eating cereal for breakfast instead of eggs. It also was conducted using dried egg yolk powder instead of whole eggs. Dried egg yolk powder is much different from freshly cooked eggs because the fats in the yolk are altered during the drying process. The bottom line is that no studies have ever found an increase in deaths from heart disease—or proven any other kinds of dangers—from eating freshly cooked eggs.*

152 ▪ **Scramble eggs or egg whites with flavorful fresh herbs and vegetables.** Combinations like fresh basil, parsley, and chopped green onion—or diced tomatoes with Italian seasoning—definitely give new salt-free taste twists to ordinary scrambled eggs. *One Salt Shaker.*

153 ▪ **Use lower-sodium natural cheeses like Swiss, baby Swiss, or mozzarella** in omelettes, frittatas, and other egg dishes and use them sparingly (about one ounce per serving). *Two to Three Salt Shakers.*

154 ▪ **Or lower the sodium content further** by using sodium-reduced cheese. *One to Two Salt Shakers.*

155 ▪ **Or eliminate cheese altogether** and use lots of vegetables for flavor. *One Salt Shaker.*

156 ▪ **Skip breakfast meats like ham, bacon, Canadian bacon, and sausage.** These foods are high in salt and sugar, which both contribute to heart disease. They also contain sodium nitrite, which is known to increase the risk of stomach cancer.

▪ BONUS TIP: *I highly recommend eliminating breakfast meats for optimal health. If you decide to eat them occasionally, however, choose a brand with the lowest amount of salt, sugar, and additives that you can find, and be sure to take 1,000 milligrams of supplemental vitamin C when you eat them. Vitamin C has been shown to block some of the carcinogenic effects that sodium nitrite can cause in the body.*

157 ▪ **If you long for sausage, make your own.** By combining ground turkey with herbs and spices, you get lots of flavor in homemade sausage patties, but much less fat and sodium—and no salt, sugar, or additives. *One Salt Shaker.*

▪ ▪ ▪

▪ LOW-SODIUM TURKEY SAUSAGE* ▪

2 pounds lean ground turkey (Shelton's brand preferred)
1 tablespoon dried sage, crushed
1 teaspoon garlic powder
1 teaspoon onion powder
1 teaspoon ground mace
1 teaspoon freshly ground black pepper
1/4 teaspoon ground allspice
1/4 teaspoon ground cloves

Combine all the ingredients in a large mixing bowl. Mix thoroughly and form into 12 patties. Bake [at 350°] or broil on both sides until done. *Makes 12 patties.*

▪ BONUS TIP: *Make these patties ahead and freeze them in individual plastic bags, as cookbook author Jeanne Jones likes to do. If you do this, you have handy, individual, low-sodium sausage patties that can be ready in a flash.*

CEREALS AND MILKS TO TOP THEM

158 ▪ **Seek out low-sodium or very-low-sodium ready-to-eat cereals.** Hidden in some of the healthiest-looking cereals is sodium in every disguised form imaginable. Since cereals are made with grains (and sometimes with dried fruits and nuts), they should contain very little sodium. Most commercial brands, however, are made with so much salt and sodium

* This recipe was adapted from a recipe for Low-Sodium Sausage that appeared in *Secrets of Salt-Free Cooking* by Jeanne Jones.

preservatives that they often contain between 200 to 300 milligrams or more of sodium per serving. (A $^3/_4$-cup serving of Ralston Wheat Chex contains 390 milligrams!) Review the list of sodium names in tip 78 before you shop for cereals, and don't be fooled by cereals that look healthy just because they are labeled "low-fat" or "fat-free." Many of these cereals supply more sodium per ounce than potato chips! When in doubt, stick with basics like salt-free, sugar-free, low-fat shredded wheat or oatmeal. *One Salt Shaker.*

159 ▪ **Take a trip to your local natural food store** to find healthier, lower-sodium alternatives to your favorite cereals. If you start your day with Kellogg's Corn Flakes, the most popular cereal worldwide, I bet you didn't know that you consume 300 milligrams of sodium in every one-cup serving. If you make just one change—switch to Arrowhead Mills Corn Flakes—you'll reduce your sodium intake at breakfast by 80 percent! (In addition, you'll eat a cereal made with organically produced corn and sweeteners and one that is preserved with vitamins C and E instead of harmful BHA and BHT.) *One Salt Shaker.*

160 ▪ **Choose hot, whole-grain cereals that have no salt added.** Once again, Arrowhead Mills is a good brand. It makes a complete line of organically produced hot cereals that are sodium-free. *One Salt Shaker.*

161 ▪ **Make hot cereals with little or no salt,** even though package instructions usually call for it. If you make regular oatmeal without salt instead of with salt, the savings in unnecessary sodium is substantial: one milligram instead of 374. *One Salt Shaker.*

162 ▪ **Add dried herbs or herb seeds to hot cereal instead of salt.** One addition that will delight the senses is crushed anise seeds or caraway seeds in cooked cream of rye cereal. *One Salt Shaker.*

163 ▪ Also try chopped fruits and toasted, chopped nuts in hot cereal. These additions are tasty and filled with nutrients but extremely low in sodium. Fruits and nuts also can be mixed and matched in many different ways to create inventive, enjoyable cereals. One client of mine likes to start her day with oatmeal topped with chopped apple, toasted walnuts, and a light sprinkling of cinnamon. Another one opts for cooked cream of brown rice cereal mixed with plenty of flavorful toasted pecans and a few raisins. *One Salt Shaker.*

CHAPTER 4

Get the Salt Out
of Soups and Salads

Soups and salads are handy foods. They can be snacks, starters before a main course, or meals in themselves. They also can range in flavor from cool to mild to spicy hot. Salads can satisfy our need to crunch and chew, while soups are the ultimate comfort foods, allowing us to sip easy-to-digest liquid nutrition.

At their best, soups and salads showcase the wonderful flavor and nutrition of fresh vegetables (and sometimes of fresh meat and grains) with very little sodium. At their worst, however, soups and salads are salt-laden nutritional disasters disguised as healthful foods. The difference depends on what kinds of ingredients go into your soup pot or salad bowl. Is the soup made from low-sodium homemade stock or high-sodium commercial stock? Are a variety of fresh vegetables and herbs added to flavor the soup, or loads of salt and sodium-containing ingredients that sound as if they belong in a chemistry experiment? Is the dressing on your fresh low-sodium salad a homemade vinaigrette or a store-bought blue cheese? Start asking yourself questions like these and you will be well on your way to mastering the challenge of getting the salt out of soups and salads.

Reducing salt in soups and salads while enhancing their flavor is a little-known art. In this day and age when reducing fat is the main health buzz Americans hear, extra salt is often added to soups and salads for flavor. The tips in this chapter will help teach you the secrets of how to make soups and salads with less salt but plenty of zest.

TAKING STOCK

164 ▪ **Good stock** can make the difference between extraordinarily tasty soup and mediocre soup. Unfortunately, most stock used in today's cooking is only given flavor with outrageous amounts of refined salt. To avoid all that salt—as well as the MSG so common in commercial stock—make your own. Here's an idea for an easy-to-prepare, savory stock based simply on herbs. It comes from George R. Schwartz, author of *In Bad Taste: The MSG Syndrome. One Salt Shaker.*

▪ QUICK HERB STOCK ▪

2 tablespoons dried thyme
2 tablespoons dried parsley
1 tablespoon dried oregano
10 black peppercorns, crushed
4 bay leaves
1 medium onion, sliced thin
2 quarts cold water

Place all the ingredients in a soup pot. Bring to a boil and simmer until the liquid is reduced by half. Pass through a fine strainer and cool. Refrigerate or freeze. *Makes 1 quart.*

165 ▪ **Save the peels and trimmings from vegetables you chop during the week** and use them to make one-of-a-kind vegetable stock. Those vegetable peelings may be "leftovers," but the broth they can produce is first-rate. Be sure to include the skins of vegetables like onions in the stock. These little-used parts of vegetables are secrets for imparting extra flavor without the salt. To make vegetable stock, add to a soup pot whatever vegetable odds and ends that you have (for example, well-washed celery leaves, onion skins, carrot trimmings, cauliflower leaves, broccoli stalks, etc.). Add at least twice as much water as vegetable pieces, bring to a boil, then reduce the heat and simmer, covered, for an hour. Strain the stock through a triple-mesh strainer and press the vegetables to release their juices. Cool and refrigerate or separate into individual containers and freeze. Yield will vary based on the amount of vegetables and water added. *One Salt Shaker.*

166 ▪ **Add ¼ to ½ cup dry white wine and one bouquet garni to the stock pot for extra flavor.** To make a bouquet garni, combine herbs like bay leaf, a few sprigs of parsley, and a sprig of thyme and wrap them in a tied cheesecloth or put them in a metal tea ball. Add to your stock and simmer. *One Salt Shaker.*

167 ▪ **Add garlic to your stock or, better yet, make Garlic Broth** to use as a fabulous base for bean or vegetable soups. Garlic, of course, packs a powerful flavoring punch and is well known for its ability to lower high blood pressure and high cholesterol levels, enhance the immune system, and ward off bacteria, yeasts, and fungi. The following recipe for Garlic Broth was developed by Holly Sollars. By using this broth in cooking, you have not only an enjoyable way of using less salt but also a handy way of receiving garlic's remarkable medicinal benefits. *One Salt Shaker.*

▪ GARLIC BROTH ▪

5 to 6 unpeeled garlic cloves
4 carrots, cut in half, then cut into eighths
3 celery stalks, cut in half, then cut into eighths
1 small onion with skin on, cut into eighths
$1/2$ bunch fresh parsley (no need to chop)
$1/4$ teaspoon black pepper
5 fresh thyme sprigs (optional)
3 bay leaves

Combine all the ingredients with 16 cups of water in a large pot over high heat. Bring to a boil, then reduce the heat, cover, and simmer for about an hour. Pour the stock through a strainer into a heat-resistant container. Press as much liquid from the vegetables as possible. Cool the stock, then refrigerate or freeze. *Makes approximately 1 gallon.*

168 ▪ **If you're a real garlic lover,** add some additional garlic to broth at the last minute. For example, to give the above recipe for Garlic Broth an even richer garlic flavor, take another half a head of garlic and peel and slice the cloves. Sauté the sliced cloves in one tablespoon of olive oil for three to four minutes, then mix it into the broth. Allow the broth to cool as directed. *One Salt Shaker.*

▪ BONUS TIP: *After having Garlic Broth or anything else made with garlic, chew on a sprig of fresh, chlorophyll-rich parsley to freshen your breath naturally.*

169 ▪ **To make a rich meat broth without the salt,** brown beef, veal, or lamb bones in a 400-degree oven for an hour before transferring them to a soup pot and adding water to simmer them. This process seems to allow more of the rich meat flavor to come through in the broth. Cook the broth for two to three hours or more. (Longer cooking produces a more flavorful stock. If enough water is used, the stock can be simmered for as long as eight hours.) When the broth has reduced enough, strain it, cool, and refrigerate or freeze. *One Salt Shaker.*

170 ▪ Condense low-sodium broth to concentrate its flavor. If simmering poultry parts for 1¹/₂ hours produces a broth that's too bland for your taste buds, try this stronger version. *One Salt Shaker.*

▪ CONDENSED CHICKEN OR TURKEY STOCK* ▪

3 pounds chicken or turkey parts (wings, backs, necks, and giblets work well)
2 celery stalks, sliced
2 carrots, peeled and sliced
1 large onion, peeled and quartered
2 parsley sprigs
2 bay leaves

Put all the ingredients in a large pot with a lid and add enough cold low-sodium water to cover by 1 inch. Bring slowly to a boil. Once it boils, reduce the heat, cover, and simmer for 1¹/₂ hours. Remove the poultry parts and vegetables and strain the stock. Return the stock to the pot and cook longer until the stock is reduced by about 25 percent. (This makes the broth richer.) Set the stock aside to cool, then refrigerate overnight or until the fat has solidified on top. Remove the fat and store the stock in the freezer in containers that are the size you use most frequently. *Makes about 6 cups.*

---

* This recipe was adapted from a recipe for Basic Chicken or Turkey Stock that appeared in my book *Get the Sugar Out* (Crown, 1996).

171 ▪ A tasty addition to stock is defatted poultry or meat drippings. When you bake a chicken or a roast, simply pour any remaining juices into a jar or covered cup. Chill it until the fat hardens into a solid white layer, then scrape it off. Use this defatted, concentrated juice for extra richness in any salt-free broth. *One Salt Shaker.*

172 ▪ Keep low-sodium canned broth at home for those times when you are too busy to make broth from scratch. Brands to look for include Hain's Healthy Naturals No-Salt-Added Vegetable Broth or Chicken Broth, Shelton's Low-Sodium Chicken Broth, and Health Valley No-Salt-Added Chicken Broth. *One Salt Shaker.*

173 ▪ If low-sodium canned broth tastes bland, jazz it up by simmering it with flavorful herbs and vegetables and reducing it a bit. In the following recipe, Harriet Roth, author of *Deliciously Simple*, puts this helpful tip into action. She also passes along another important suggestion: freeze broth into ice cubes to make low-salt cooking faster and even more convenient. *One Salt Shaker.*

▪ CHICKEN BOUILLON CUBES ▪

2 (10^1/$_2$-ounce) cans salt-free chicken broth, defatted
^{1}/$_2$ cup dry white wine or vermouth
2 shallots, chopped
1 teaspoon herbes de Provence or dried thyme, crushed

Combine all the ingredients in a 1-quart saucepan. Simmer until reduced to 1^1/$_2$ cups. Pour into an ice cube tray and freeze. Remove from the tray and seal in plastic bags. (Do not wet the cubes or they will stick together.) *Makes 12 cubes.*

174 ▪ Don't use bouillon cubes or bouillon powder. They're staggeringly high in salt and sodium and frequently contain hidden MSG. Avoid even the low-sodium varieties; they contain sodium-based additives and other undesirable chemicals.

175 ▪ **Instead, to make broth quickly use unsalted stock concentrates.** Perfect Addition is a brand that can be found in the frozen foods section of some health food stores. With wholesome ingredients like fresh vegetables, herbs, and wine, the beef, chicken, fish, and vegetable stocks made by this company are low in sodium but very rich. To make a broth with them, simply combine them with equal amounts of water. What could be simpler? *One Salt Shaker.*

SOUP BASICS

176 ▪ **Use any of the already mentioned stocks as a base,** then add additional vegetables and poultry or meat pieces to create low-salt soups and stews with hearty flavor. Other ingredients that help make soups tasty include:

177 ▪ **Leftover liquid from cooked beans.** *One Salt Shaker.*

178 ▪ **Pureed cooked vegetables like onions and peppers.** *One Salt Shaker.*

179 ▪ **Defatted gravies.** *One Salt Shaker.*

180 ▪ **Leftover liquid used to soak dried mushrooms or dried tomatoes.** *One Salt Shaker.*

181 ▪ **It's best to salt soup to taste *after* cooking,** but if you do accidentally oversalt your soup during cooking, you can remedy the situation this way: add a peeled and quartered raw potato to the soup, then let the soup simmer for ten to fifteen minutes. The excess salt will absorb into the potato, and you simply can remove and discard the potato.

182 ▪ **Sauté chopped vegetables in a few teaspoons of oil or butter first** before adding to soups. The fat used for sautéing brings out the flavor in vegetables more than fat-free broth, which almost always requires extra salt for flavor. *One Salt Shaker.*

183 ▪ **Miso (see tip 65) is a natural for giving a simple vegetable soup more of a salty taste.** But refrain from using this condiment in excess: a teaspoon of miso for every cup of water or stock is usually sufficient to flavor soup without using too much salt. To add miso to soup, dilute it in $1/4$ cup of broth from the soup, mix it well, then add it to the soup and simmer for another minute. Serve immediately. *Two Salt Shakers.*

184 ▪ **Try adding a teaspoon of minced fresh lovage leaf** to a pot of salt-free soup just before serving. Lovage leaf is an herbal salt substitute that has a flavor somewhat reminiscent of robust celery. You'll probably be surprised at how well a small amount of this little-known herb can heighten flavor. Look for fresh lovage leaf in the produce section of upscale supermarkets or buy a plant or some seeds and grow your own. *One Salt Shaker.*

185 ▪ **Give soups surprising flavor contrasts** to keep your taste buds so interested that they'll forget about salt. That's exactly what Sal Gilbertie, author of *Kitchen Herbs*, does in this recipe. By using varied ingredients like chile peppers, lime juice, lemongrass, and fresh cilantro, he creates an aromatic hot-tart soup with a cooling, refreshing garnish. Even more impressive, this gourmet soup tastes as if it should take a long time to make, but it's exceedingly simple and quick to prepare. *Two Salt Shakers.*

▪ ▪ ▪

■ SPICY THAI SHRIMP SOUP
WITH FRESH CILANTRO ■

3 quarts homemade chicken stock
2 (6-inch) fresh lemongrass stalks, sliced
1 to 2 red chile peppers, seeded and thinly sliced
Zest of 1 lime
1/2 pound fresh straw mushrooms
1 pound large shrimp (12 to 15 per pound), shelled and
    deveined
2/3 cup fresh lime juice
4 scallions, sliced
1/2 cup chopped fresh cilantro

In a large soup pot, combine the broth, lemongrass, chile peppers, and lime zest. Bring to a boil; cover and simmer for 15
minutes. Lift out the lime zest and discard. Add the mushrooms and shrimp; simmer for 4 minutes. Stir in the lime juice.
Transfer the shrimp to a serving bowl and pour in the broth.
Sprinkle with the scallions and cilantro. *Serves 4.*

**186 ■ For convenience, look for no-salt soup mixes or
make your own.** Popular commercial soup starters and instant
cups of soup may be handy, but they actually are small salt
mines, often containing more than 500 milligrams of sodium
and sometimes as much as 1,000 milligrams per cup! To avoid
all that salt, plan ahead and make this simple Speedy Soup Mix.
It will allow you the same no-fuss soup preparation commercial
soup starters do, but with five to ten times less sodium. This
versatile recipe is another one from *Deliciously Simple* by Harriet Roth. *One Salt Shaker.*

■ ■ ■

▪ SPEEDY SOUP MIX ▪

$1/4$ cup small white beans or lima beans
$1/4$ cup red kidney beans or pinto beans
$1/4$ cup green or yellow split peas or lentils
$1/4$ cup barley or brown rice
3 tablespoons dehydrated onion flakes
3 tablespoons freeze-dried chopped shallot
$1/2$ teaspoon garlic flakes
$1/4$ cup freeze-dried mushrooms
3 tablespoons dehydrated vegetable flakes
1 bay leaf
$1/2$ teaspoon crushed salt-free vegetable seasoning
1 teaspoon dried Italian herb blend or herbes de Provence,
   crushed

To store, combine all the ingredients and place in a covered container or plastic bag. *Makes 2 cups dry mix.* To prepare, combine 1 recipe dry soup mix with 8 cups of water or salt-free chicken, turkey, or vegetable broth in a 4-quart saucepan. Bring to a boil and simmer for 1 to $1^{1}/2$ hours, or until the beans are tender. Taste and adjust the seasonings. Remove bay leaf before serving.

187 ▪ Don't be fooled by canned soup labels that *sound* good for you. Remember that manufacturers often try to cleverly label foods to capitalize on consumers' interest in eating better. Here are a few examples. Campbell's Home Cookin' Minestrone certainly sounds as if it should be full of goodness, but hydrolyzed wheat gluten, yeast extract, MSG, and 990 milligrams of sodium aren't what most people expect in a cup of good, old-fashioned, home-cooked soup. Healthy Choice makes a country vegetable soup that delivers on its lower-sodium claims, but with 430 milligrams per cup it's still not exactly *low* in sodium. (In addition, it contains unwanted sugar, maltodextrin, and added color.) Campbell's Healthy Request Minestrone is labeled MSG-free—which it is—but it also contains disodium inosinate and disodium guanylate, which are potent flavor enhancers that may cause adverse physical reactions similar to what MSG does. Don't forget that the foods that are best for you come without a label. If this easy-to-make Spring Minestrone from my book *Super Nutrition for Menopause* had a label, its claims would be impressive: home-cooked, healthy style, low in fat, low in sodium, sugar-free, MSG-free and preservative-free! *One to Two Salt Shakers.*

■ SPRING MINESTRONE ■

1 onion, sliced
1 teaspoon canola oil
2 celery stalks, chopped
3 medium carrots, sliced
1 cup green beans, cut into 1-inch pieces
1 cup sweet peas
1 teaspoon fresh marjoram
1 teaspoon fresh thyme
2 tablespoons chopped fresh parsley
1 cup broccoli florets
1 medium potato, cubed
1 cup mushrooms, sliced
1 strip kombu (see tip 61) (optional)
$1/4$ teaspoon salt (optional)

Sauté the onion in oil over low heat until translucent. Add $1^{1}/_{2}$ quarts of water and bring to a boil. Add all the other vegetables and herbs and stir for 1 minute. Cover and simmer for 20 to 30 minutes. (Remove the kombu, if used.) Season with salt, if desired. *Serves 6.*

188 ▪ **Keep Hain Healthy Naturals No-Salt-Added Soups on hand** to have when you're sick or just too busy to cook. Remember, it's fine to add some Real Salt or sea salt at the table if you need to. *One to Two Salt Shakers.*

SALAD DAYS

189 ▪ **Enjoy fresh lettuce salads** to your heart's content. Whether you eat a plain mixed green salad or one chock full of a variety of crunchy vegetables, salads are naturally low in sodium, not to mention rich in nutrients like beta-carotene, vitamin C, and potassium. *One Salt Shaker.*
  ▪ BONUS TIP: *Choose darker green lettuce like romaine or red or green leaf over iceberg lettuce whenever possible. Although iceberg lettuce is more familiar to many people than its darker green cousins, it is nutritionally inferior (especially in potassium and folic acid). If you can't forgo iceberg lettuce right away, gradually mix more dark green lettuce leaves into your regular mix to increase your salad's nutritional content.*
  190 ▪ **Don't be afraid to eat spinach salad,** even though spinach is higher in sodium than lettuce. One cup of raw, chopped spinach still contains only 44 milligrams of sodium, which is well within this book's *One Salt Shaker* definition. (Besides, spinach is beneficial in other important ways: it is the richest source of hard-to-get lutein, a nutrient that can prevent age-related eye diseases as we get older.)

191 ▪ **Before adding salad greens to your bowl,** rub the bowl with half a garlic clove. The garlic essence that is rubbed in will heighten the taste of your greens. *One Salt Shaker.*

192 ▪ **Top salad greens with minced fresh herbs** ranging from familiar basil and oregano to unusual herbs like chervil. Each one gives salad a refreshingly different flavor. *One Salt Shaker.*

193 ▪ **Experiment with pesticide-free, edible flowers on salad.** They add aroma and flavor to food, and their bright colors are beautiful and springlike against a "field" of greens. Good flowers to try on salads are any herbs that have bloomed; they have peppery, herbal flavors that are nice additions. Leave small blossoms whole, but cut large flowers into small pieces. Here are some that are especially tasty or pretty: hyssop and anise hyssop; borage; rosemary; thyme; sage; lavender; oregano; scented geraniums; chive, onion, and garlic blossoms; cilantro (coriander); citrus flowers; and nasturtiums. *One Salt Shaker.*

194 ▪ **Add pungent "bite" to your salad** with fiery radish, chopped red onion, or a garnish of jalapeño pepper. Any of these tastes will keep your taste buds electrified. *One Salt Shaker.*

195 ▪ **Become a peppercorn connoisseur:** change the taste of salads by cracking different varieties of peppercorns in your pepper mill. From traditional black Malabar peppercorns to green, pink, or white peppercorns, these zesty seasonings are fun to experiment with on salads, especially when you're reducing the salt in your diet. *One Salt Shaker.*

196 ▪ **Like croutons on your salad?** Few people realize a tremendous amount of salt lurks in those tasty morsels. Fortunately, you still can enjoy seasoned croutons on your salad as long as you make them at home without the salt. They're pretty simple to make: lightly toast low-sodium, whole-grain bread, then rub it with a garlic clove while it's still warm. (The garlic will "melt" into the bread.) Sprinkle with any herbs or herbal blends of your choice, then cut into cubes and toast on a baking sheet in a 350-degree oven until crisp. *One Salt Shaker.*

197 ▪ **Crumbled feta cheese is a popular salad topper,** but native Greeks will tell you that freshly made feta cheese is never as salty as the packaged feta cheese Americans are accustomed to. You still can enjoy feta cheese on salads; just get most of the salt out of it first. To lower the sodium content of feta cheese, soak the amount of cheese you want to use in low-sodium water for about five minutes, drain it, and lightly pat it dry with a paper towel. Much of the salt will be removed, but the delicious goat-cheese flavor will remain. *One Salt Shaker.*

198 ▪ **To make salad into a meal,** top it with leftover, plain-cooked chicken, turkey, or beef slices, or low-sodium canned tuna. *One Salt Shaker.*

199 ▪ **For a vegetarian alternative,** top salad with low-sodium canned chickpeas. *One Salt Shaker.*

200 ▪ **If you have high blood pressure,** be sure to add chopped celery to your salad. Although celery is one of the highest vegetable sources of sodium, it is still low in sodium. In addition, it has another bonus: it contains a compound called 3-n-butyl phthalide, which is known to lower high blood pressure. Several holistic doctors such as Michael T. Murray, author of *Natural Alternatives to Over-the-counter and Prescription Drugs* (William Morrow and Company, 1994), suggest that hypertensive individuals eat four celery stalks per day. *One Salt Shaker.*

201 ▪ **Transform any leftover vegetables into an elegant salad.** It's easy to do when you follow this recipe from Harriet Roth's cookbook *Deliciously Low. One Salt Shaker.*

▪ ▪ ▪

▪ YESTERDAY'S VEGETABLES BECOME TODAY'S SALAD ▪

Any low-sodium, sugar-free vinaigrette dressing
Leftover bits of raw or cooked vegetables
Fresh lettuce leaves of your choice

Put the vinaigrette dressing in a generous-size jar. Each day, add any leftover bits of raw or cooked vegetables except for salad greens. In a few days, lift the marinated vegetable mixture with a slotted spoon onto fresh lettuce leaves and serve as a delicious salad. You will discover unusual and flavorful mixtures this way. *Yield will vary, based on the amount of vegetables used.*

202 ▪ Dry mixes for grain salads like tabouli may be easy to use, but even the packaged brands carried in health food stores contain entirely too much salt. To have some of the convenience dry mixes offer without all that unnecessary sodium, use leftover cooked grains or quick-cooking grains to quickly prepare grain salads. In this recipe, nutritionist Melissa Diane Smith combines quick-cooking bulgur wheat with bountiful fresh ingredients for a real herbal experience: a refreshing Middle Eastern tabouli salad that takes only about 30 minutes to prepare. *One Salt Shaker.*

▪ FRESH HERBAL TABOULI ▪

1 cup bulgur wheat
1 cup plus 2 tablespoons boiling water
3 tablespoons Spectrum World Cuisine Mediterranean
    Oil *or* other garlic herbed oil (or extra-virgin olive oil)
$1/3$ to $1/2$ cup fresh lemon juice (to your taste)
2 garlic cloves, minced

1 cup finely chopped fresh parsley
1/3 cup finely chopped fresh mint
1 to 3 chopped scallions
2 tablespoons finely chopped fresh basil (optional)
2 tomatoes, diced (optional)
1 cucumber, peeled, seeded, and diced (optional)
1/8 teaspoon Herbamare herbal salt (optional)

Place the wheat in a bowl, pour the boiling water over it, and leave to soak for 30 minutes to soften. (It should absorb all the water.) While the bulgur is soaking, combine the oil and lemon juice together with the minced garlic. When the bulgur is ready, add all of the herbs and vegetables and lemon juice–oil mixture to it and mix well. If there's time, allow to chill for several hours for the best flavor. *Serves 6.*

203 ▪ **What's sauerkraut without salt?** Both very delicious and extremely healthful. When you make sauerkraut the traditional way, you need a little bit of patience to wait for the results, but the rewards you receive are well worth it—fresh flavor, lots of nutrients, and beneficial enzymes that promote healthy digestion. Use raw sauerkraut as a salad or as a cold side dish to go with sandwiches or oven-fried chicken. *One Salt Shaker.*

▪ ▪ ▪

▪ SALT-FREE SAUERKRAUT* ▪

2 heads green cabbage and 1 head red cabbage
1 to 2 onions, chopped (optional)
1 to 2 celery stalks, chopped (optional)
2 tablespoons celery seeds, crushed or ground (optional)
2 tablespoons caraway seeds, crushed (optional)
2 tablespoons dill weed or dill seeds, crushed (optional)
1 teaspoon ground kelp [see tip 60] (optional)
1 tablespoon garlic powder (optional)
$^1/_2$ to $^3/_4$ cup freshly squeezed lemon juice (optional)

Pull off the outer leaves of the cabbage and grate the rest. Put the grated cabbage in one mixing bowl, the other vegetables in a second bowl, and the ground herbs, spices, and lemon juice, if using, in a third bowl. Pound the cabbage lightly with a wooden tenderizing mallet. Put a layer of the cabbage a few inches deep in a crock or in a glass or stainless steel pot. Add a similar layer of the vegetable mixture over the cabbage and pack it down. Then sprinkle with the spices or some of the spice–lemon juice mixture. Continue the process with more layers until you are finished with the ingredients and press down each layer so the vegetables will be saturated in their own juice. Allow at least a few inches of space from the top of the pot because the fermenting vegetables are likely to expand. Cover the vegetable mixture on top with the outer leaves of the cabbage, tucking the leaves around the mixture as completely as you can. Put a plate on top that fits nicely in the crock. Then add a weight or a filled glass jar on top of the plate. Place a clean dish towel over the crock and let the fermenting vegetables sit in a well-ventilated room at room temperature for 5

---

* This recipe was adapted from a sauerkraut recipe entitled Our Favorite Beginner's Recipe in *The Body Ecology Diet* by Donna Gates.

to 7 days. After 5 to 7 days, throw away the old cabbage leaves and any moldy or discolored vegetables on top. Put the remaining sauerkraut in glass jars and refrigerate. This sauerkraut will last a few months in the refrigerator if the glass jars are opened minimally. *Yields several quarts.*

DRESSED FOR SUCCESS

204 ▪ **The biggest problem with salads,** of course, isn't the vegetables that go in them, but the commercial salad dressings that are put on top of them. If you use two tablespoons of a dressing that contain 200 milligrams of sodium per tablespoon, you consume one-fifth of the total amount of sodium I recommend for most individuals in a single day. What's worse, the sodium in commercial dressings is unhealthy, being derived from common table salt and sodium additives and preservatives. To keep a healthful salad from turning into a meal with loads of unhealthy sodium, buy low-sodium dressings that are made with sea salt and that do not contain sodium preservatives. *One Salt Shaker.*

205 ▪ **Or buy unsalted dressings** like Cardini's No Salt Added varieties. You always can add natural salt (either unrefined sea salt, Real Salt, sesame salt, herbal salt, or kelp powder) on your own if you need to. (See tips 54, 55, 58, 59, and 60.) *One to Two Salt Shakers.*

206 ▪ **When in doubt, use vinegar and olive oil or lemon juice and olive oil for a dressing.** Either of these are simple but tangy ways to top your salad without salt. *One Salt Shaker.*

207 ▪ **Use salt-free herbal blends or different medleys of dried herbs** to vary the flavor of either of these basic dressings. *One Salt Shaker.*

208 ▪ **Utilize the pungent power of garlic in salad dressings.** Garlic is a wonder food, providing plenty of flavor as well as abundant health benefits. In this recipe from *The Healing Power of Foods Cookbook* by Michael T. Murray, N.D., garlic is combined with a variety of fresh and dried herbs to create a delightfully tasty Herb Dressing. *One Salt Shaker.*

▪ HERB DRESSING ▪

6 tablespoons vegetable oil
2 teaspoons chopped fresh parsley
2 teaspoons chopped fresh chives
2 tablespoons chopped fresh chervil *or* 2 teaspoons dried
   chervil
Black pepper to taste
$1/2$ cup rice vinegar
2 tablespoons water
3 garlic cloves, minced
2 teaspoons dried mustard

In a blender, combine all the ingredients and blend thoroughly. *Serves 8 (2 tablespoons per serving).*

209 ▪ **Add a gourmet touch to everyday salad:** use herbed vinegar or herbed oil, either by itself or in combination. (See tips 44, 45, and 46.) When the essence of delightfully fragrant herbs graces every drop of vinegar or oil that you sprinkle, you'll be amazed at how much less dressing you need to use for flavor. *One Salt Shaker.*

210 ▪ **Also experiment with different kinds of unrefined oils.** When you buy a high-quality oil, the aroma and taste of the nut, seed, or plant from which the oil is derived should come through loud and strong. If the brand of oil you use is bland and not distinct, no matter whether you buy almond, sesame, or olive oil, you're probably buying an oil that has been bleached and deodorized. In fact, it may be so processed that it is actually harmful to the body. Switch to using oils labeled "unrefined" in salad dressings and get the healthy fats, vitamin E, and distinctive flavor that you've been missing. This recipe from my book *Beyond Pritikin* uses the unique nutty flavor of sesame oil. *One to Two Salt Shakers.*

▪ SESAME-LEMON DRESSING ▪

$1/2$ cup light sesame oil
1 tablespoon fresh lemon juice
$1/2$ teaspoon grated fresh lemon zest
$1/4$ teaspoon salt (optional)
$1/2$ teaspoon dried dill

Combine all the ingredients in a covered jar and shake well. Refrigerate. *Serves 8.*

211 ▪ **Try mustard oil,** which is available at East Indian stores and some specialty food markets. Usually used in combination with other ingredients, this pungent oil is a fantastic help for dressing lettuce- or bean-based salads with flavor but no salt. *One Salt Shaker.*

212 ▪ **Don't forget about garlic oil,** a natural to use on salads. (To make a quick garlic oil, blend garlic with extra-virgin olive oil in a blender.) Combine garlic oil with fresh lemon juice or apple cider vinegar to create an enjoyable and very healthful dressing. *One Salt Shaker.*

213 ▪ **Another salt-free condiment is chili oil,** which you can find in the Oriental section of most health food stores and upscale supermarkets. Just a splash or two of hot chili oil combined with fresh lime juice makes a wonderful dressing for bean salads. *One Salt Shaker.*

214 ▪ **Salt-free tomato sauce and tomato juice** are two other versatile salad dressing ingredients. By changing the herbs and other ingredients you combine with them, you can create everything from a tomato-basil Italian vinaigrette to a hot and chunky, Mexican salsa-style dressing. Here Harriet Roth, the author of *Deliciously Low,* uses salt-free tomato sauce in combination with yogurt to make a creamy Russian dressing. *One Salt Shaker.*

▪ MY FAVORITE RUSSIAN DRESSING ▪

1 cup nonfat yogurt
$1/4$ cup salt-free tomato sauce
2 hard-boiled egg whites, chopped
$1/4$ cup diced green pepper
$1/2$ teaspoon onion powder
$1/4$ teaspoon garlic powder
$1/4$ teaspoon low-sodium vegetable seasoning
Dash of Tabasco

Place all the ingredients into a bowl and blend well with a whisk. *Makes $1^1/2$ cups.*

215 ▪ **If you're used to salty dressings,** gradually wean yourself away from them by diluting them with water or lemon juice to lessen the saltiness. *Two Salt Shakers.*

216 ▪ **Apply the same concept to creamy dressings that are overly salty:** thin them out with plain nonfat yogurt. *Two Salt Shakers.*

217 ▪ **Beware of fat-free dressings,** which often have extra salt (and sometimes extra sugar) to compensate for the flavor the fat used to provide. If you pile on the fat-free ranch dressing because it's "fat free," you should know that a two-tablespoon serving of Hidden Valley Original Ranch Dressing contains 260 milligrams of sodium, but the same amount of Hidden Valley Fat-Free Ranch contains 320 milligrams. That additional unhealthy sodium will add up every time you eat a salad. To avoid all that salt, try this recipe from *The American Heart Association Low-Salt Cookbook*. It will show you how to get much of the unnecessary fat out of ranch dressing without adding extra sodium. *Two Salt Shakers.*

▪ REDUCED CALORIE RANCH DRESSING ▪

1 cup buttermilk
$1/2$ cup plain low-fat yogurt
1 tablespoon Dijon mustard
2 teaspoons minced onion
1 tablespoon fresh dill
1 tablespoon chopped fresh parsley
$1/2$ teaspoon garlic powder
$1/4$ teaspoon freshly ground black pepper

In a jar with a tight-fitting lid, combine all the ingredients. Shake well to blend. Refrigerate for at least 2 hours, allowing the flavors to blend. *Makes $1^1/_2$ cups.*

218 ▪ If you're used to making a dressing from a mix, did you know that salt is often a major ingredient in almost all of those handy mixes? It is, unless you've already discovered a brand like The Spice Hunter, which makes a complete line of mixes that are both salt- and sugar-free. *One Salt Shaker.*

CHAPTER 5

Get the Salt Out
of Entrées and Side Dishes

Getting the salt out of meals can be done a number of different ways. Judging from my experience as a professional nutritionist, I would say that most people who are told to eat a low-sodium diet go about it in exactly the wrong manner. They pay little attention to whether different foods supply good or bad forms of sodium and often assume the lower the sodium, the better. As a result, they tend to emphasize nutrient-poor, low-sodium white bread and white pasta and to use convenience products like low-sodium bouillon cubes that have few recognizable food ingredients.

When you add the antifat propaganda that has swept across our land, many people who are trying to reduce their salt intake also give up nutritious foods like zinc-rich beef and seafood, and some avoid animal protein altogether. Their overzealous and unhealthy fat phobia also causes them to avoid magnesium- and potassium-rich nuts and seeds, and to avoid using even the tiniest amount of healthy oil in cooking. The result is a group of well-intentioned individuals who give up salt for health reasons but who develop across-the-board deficiencies of certain nutrients, which lead to far worse health problems than they had before.

The key to reducing dietary salt healthfully does not involve eating uninspiring, unbalanced meals or relying on unpalatable "fake" foods that are low in sodium but have virtually no other nutritional value. Quite to the contrary, the secret must involve keeping as many healthy nutrients in your diet at the same time you get the unhealthy sodium out. The only way to strike this ideal balance is to take a tip from nature. When you learn how to combine natural foods creatively and choose only healthful convenience products made from natural foods, you then will have discovered the secret of how to get salt out of meals the right way.

The tips in this chapter will teach you how to do that. They'll show you that you can enjoy everything from Vegetarian Chili to Chinese stir-fries to Tandoori Chicken in less salty ways. A few of the tips also may cause you to rethink your attitudes about protein and fat, helping you to understand that receiving a balance of quality nutrients from entrées and side dishes is equally as important for health as getting the salt out.

MEATY MATTERS

219 ▪ Feel free to enjoy small portions of lean, natural meat. Although many people believe meat is high in sodium, it's not. A three-ounce portion of beef, for example, contains only between 40 and 114 milligrams of sodium (depending on the cut). Meat also supplies high-quality protein that stimulates the body's production of a fat-burning hormone and is a great source of hard-to-find zinc and iron. If you've been afraid to eat meat because you've heard it was bad for you, don't believe it: I find meat a necessary addition to many of my clients' diets.

▪ BONUS TIP: *Meat, per se, is not bad for our health, but there is no question that the antibiotics and hormones added to most commercial meat these days can be harmful. Avoid the problems these chemicals can cause by buying organically raised meats whenever possible. Look for natural meats, including chicken and turkey from Shelton's, and beef from Coleman Natural Meats.*

220 ▪ **Always choose simply prepared unprocessed meats** over processed meat products. Natural steaks, roasts, and burgers are all low in sodium and usually contain three to five times more potassium than sodium. Once meats are processed into things like hot dogs, sausage, and smoked, cured, and deli meat products, however, they are loaded with salt, and their all-important potassium-to-sodium ratio is totally reversed. Four ounces of pot roasted beef (from choice round), for example, contain 348 milligrams of potassium and 58 milligrams of sodium. Once beef is processed into four ounces of canned corned beef, though, its composition changes dramatically—to 153 milligrams of potassium and 1,139 milligrams of sodium! If you want to make a dietary change that will make a major reduction in the unnecessary sodium you consume, steer clear of processed meats. *One Salt Shaker.*

221 ▪ **Eat zinc-rich meats so you will want less salt.** Beef, lamb, chicken, and turkey are some of the best dietary sources of zinc, a mineral deficient in more than 60 percent of the American population. Research with animals has revealed that a higher preference for salt is indicated in animals who are zinc deficient than in those who are not. Zinc deficiency is known to cause a dulled sense of taste. If you are trying to cut back on the salt you consume, you can do it much more easily if you are able to lessen your desire for salt. Eating zinc-rich meats is a means to this end: it's a way to prevent zinc deficiency and, consequently, reduce the desire for salt.

▪ BONUS TIP: *The kind of protein you eat can make a big difference in how you feel. Individuals with slow metabolisms usually feel better eating lean animal products like white meat from poultry, while people with fast metabolisms tend to thrive on higher-fat lamb and beef. Try to determine which kinds of protein you feel best eating by experimenting with your diet and listening to the messages your body sends you. As I explain in* Your Body Knows Best *(Pocket Books, 1996), your body often gives you powerful physical signals about what foods are right for you.*

222 ▪ Sufficient protein-rich meat also is needed to prevent fluid imbalance, water retention, bloating, and water weight gain. Although many people blame water retention on too much salt in the diet (and sometimes on too much water), this condition is often caused by protein deficiency, a condition that is becoming increasingly common as people avoid meat and load up on carbohydrates. While too much meat in the diet can be bad for your health, too little meat can be just as harmful. Two 3-ounce portions (about the size of a deck of cards) per day is a good amount for most people.

▪ BONUS TIP: *The whole subject of meat in the diet is shrouded in confusion and misinformation. If you would like to learn more about the real pros and cons of eating meat, I suggest you consult* Your Body Knows Best, *which covers the topic in great detail.*

223 ▪ Beware of kosher meats. They're salted and their sodium content is too high for sodium-restricted diets. If you observe Jewish dietary laws, it's best to buy kosher poultry and fish, which are either not salted at all or are salted but washed three times to remove most of the salt. If you do purchase kosher meats, remove as much of the salt as possible: thoroughly wash the meats with low-sodium water, simmer them in a lot of water, and discard the cooking water. To leech as much salt as possible out of the meat, cut the meat into pieces before cooking.

224 ▪ Organ meats are higher in sodium than muscle meats, but they still don't contain nearly as much sodium as processed meats. If you occasionally enjoy eating a few pieces of nutrient-packed liver (from organic sources), prepare liver this salt-free way: lightly coat the liver pieces in whole grain flour and quickly sear them with sliced onions in a few teaspoons of canola oil until done. Then squeeze on lemon juice, add freshly cracked black pepper, and enjoy. *One Salt Shaker.*

225 ▪ Rub salt-free dry marinades into meat or poultry before grilling, broiling, or baking. With Caribbean, Barbecue, and Moroccan varieties, The Spice Hunter dry marinades are easy to use and can instantly transport your taste buds to far-away places. For the best coating and flavor, apply a very light coat of oil, broth, salt-free tomato juice, or a mixture of any of these first before shaking on and rubbing in the marinade. Then cook meat as usual. *One Salt Shaker.*

226 ▪ Give steaks and chops flavor before broiling by topping them with herbs such as oregano, rosemary, or thyme and seasonings like garlic powder or onion powder. *One Salt Shaker.*

227 ▪ Or sprinkle Robbie's low-sodium Worcestershire sauce or Mr. Spice's sodium-free Garlic Steak Sauce on them. These versatile seasonings can be found in health food stores. *One Salt Shaker.*

228 ▪ Say good-bye to Accent and other meat tenderizers that are high in sodium and frequently contain MSG. Instead, try adding blended papaya or pineapple to marinades. Both of these fruits contain enzymes that help with digestion and that also can be used to tenderize meat.

229 ▪ Other tenderizing liquids to use in marinades are wine, lemon, or lime juice, or different varieties of vinegar. If you use wine, be sure to use table wine instead of cooking wine, which has added salt. Here's a recipe from my book *Super Nutrition for Women* that uses red wine. It's tremendously flavorful, even though it has only a few ingredients. *One Salt Shaker*.

▪ SPICED BEEF WITH WINE, GINGER, AND GARLIC ▪

1 pound flank steak, all visible fat removed
$3/4$ cup dry red wine
4 teaspoons low-sodium Worcestershire sauce (see
    tip 227)
1 teaspoon powdered ginger
4 garlic cloves, mashed

Place the flank steak in a baking dish and cover with a mixture of wine, Worcestershire sauce, ginger, and garlic. Marinate for at least 2 hours in the refrigerator.

Preheat the broiler. Broil about 8 to 9 minutes on each side until done to preference. Serve hot from the oven with a salad and vegetable. *Serves 4.*

230 ▪ **Stir-fry beef or chicken strips in a small amount of herbed oil.** (See tip 44.) This is another way to impart flavor without the salt. *One Salt Shaker.*

231 ▪ **If you have to load burgers with salty ketchup and mustard to make them flavorful,** learn to put the flavor inside the burgers instead of on top of them. Elma W. Bagg does exactly that with her creation of these delightful Herbed Hamburgers from *Cooking Without a Grain of Salt. One Salt Shaker.*

▪ ▪ ▪

▪ HERBED HAMBURGER ▪

2 pounds ground lean beef (or ground round)
1 tablespoon olive oil
$1/2$ cup finely chopped onion
$1/2$ teaspoon garlic powder *or* 1 garlic clove, minced
1 tablespoon chopped fresh parsley
$1/4$ teaspoon marjoram
$1/4$ teaspoon basil
2 tablespoons fresh lemon juice
2 teaspoons cold water

Combine all the ingredients, make into 10 patties, and broil or grill until done. *Serves 10.*

232 ▪ Here's another example of how to make tasty **burgers**—give them a south-of-the-border flavor. This sassy recipe comes from *Cooking for Healthy Healing* by Linda Rector-Page. *One Salt Shaker.*

▪ MEXICAN TURKEY BURGERS ON THE GRILL ▪

1 pound ground turkey
2 tablespoons cornmeal
1 tablespoon fresh lime juice
1 jalapeño pepper, seeded and minced
2 teaspoons cumin powder
2 teaspoons salt-free chili powder
1 egg
$1/4$ teaspoon pepper

Preheat and oil the grill. Combine all the ingredients, form into 6 burgers, and grill until no longer pink in the center. Serve with salt-free salsa and a squeeze of lime. *Serves 6.*

233 ▪ **Be adventurous when using salt-free seasonings.** Just because a salt-free blend may be packaged as an onion dip mix, it doesn't mean that it isn't also a great addition to meatloaf, casseroles, or other dishes. Try using mixes in imaginative ways and see what kind of new taste twists you can add to everyday meals. *One Salt Shaker.*

234 ▪ **Avoid chicken or turkey that is "prebasted" or "deep basted."** You may not have realized it, but prebasted chicken or turkey always has extra salt added to it. It usually is injected with solutions that contain not only refined salt but also things like partially hydrogenated oil, artificial flavor, and sodium-containing preservatives. Avoid these potentially harmful ingredients by seeking out fresh, unprocessed chicken and turkey every time you shop.

235 ▪ **Also shun premarinated chicken or turkey breast cutlets.** No matter whether the poultry is marinated in lemon-herb, teriyaki, or barbecue sauce, salt is almost always one of the marinade's top ingredients.

236 ▪ **Give chicken a taste of India** by using exotic spices like ginger, coriander, cumin, and garam masala (a mixture of cinnamon, cardamom, and cloves) in marinades. If you aren't familiar with Indian food, try this simple Tandoori Chicken recipe from *Indian Recipes for a Healthy Heart* by Mrs. Lakhani. You'll discover that even without salt, Indian food is tantalizing to the taste buds. *One to Two Salt Shakers.*

▪ ▪ ▪

■ TANDOORI CHICKEN ■

2 teaspoons minced garlic
2 teaspoons minced ginger root
1 green chile, seeded and minced (optional)
$1/4$ teaspoon salt (optional)
$1/2$ teaspoon ground coriander
1 teaspoon ground cumin
$1/4$ teaspoon red chili powder (optional)
1 teaspoon garam masala
$1/2$ cup low-fat yogurt
2 tablespoons salt-free tomato paste
1 teaspoon canola oil
2 tablespoons lemon juice
4 (5-ounce) chicken breasts, skinned, with the fat removed

In a large bowl, combine all the ingredients except the chicken and make a smooth marinade. Make 2 diagonal cuts in each chicken breast and marinate for 3 to 4 hours or overnight in the refrigerator. Broil or grill chicken, occasionally basting with the marinade for 5 to 7 minutes on each side, or until cooked but not dry. *Serves 4.*

237 ■ Here's a creative way to give chicken a piquant flavor and moister texture: loosen the skin on chicken breasts or thighs and tuck a mixture of herbs in between the skin and the flesh before baking. You can create a flavorful "underskin" by using an endless variety of herb mixtures, but here is one combination I particularly like: 4 crushed garlic cloves, $1^1/2$ tablespoons grated lemon zest, and $1^1/2$ cups finely chopped parsley. Use only the amount you need for each meal, being careful to prevent any leftover herb mixture from coming in contact with the raw chicken. Remove the skin of the chicken before eating, but be sure to eat all that wonderful "underskin." *One Salt Shaker.*

238 ▪ **Learn how to reduce the sodium content of Chinese stir-fries.** One simple way is to use sodium-reduced tamari (see tip 63) in place of the standard tamari. If you have only regular tamari soy sauce, though, stretch it with salt-free ingredients like water, sherry, or unsalted broth. The Center for Science in the Public Interest did this in the following recipe for Szechuan Chicken with Peanuts from its book *Salt: The Brand Name Guide to Sodium Content.* This dish contains 302 milligrams of sodium per serving, which is a substantial reduction from the 1,000 milligrams or more per serving in traditional Szechuan-style stir-fries. *Three Salt Shakers.*

▪ SZECHUAN CHICKEN WITH PEANUTS ▪

2 whole chicken breasts, split, skinned, and boned
1 tablespoon oil
1 thin slice fresh gingerroot
1 garlic clove, peeled
3 Szechuan chile peppers, halved
$1/3$ cup unsalted peanuts
$1/2$ pound snow peas, stems removed
1 tablespoon [sodium-reduced] tamari soy sauce [see
    tip 63]
1 tablespoon dry sherry
1 teaspoon arrowroot
3 tablespoons cold water
2 scallions, cut in 1-inch pieces

Trim the fat from the chicken breasts and cut each into long, $1/2$-inch-wide strips.

Heat the oil in a wok, skillet, or sauté pan, add the ginger, garlic, and chile peppers, and cook for 2 minutes over medium heat. Add the chicken and sauté for 2 minutes, stirring constantly.

Add the peanuts, snow peas, tamari, and sherry; stir and continue cooking another minute or two.

Mix the arrowroot and water until smooth. Add the mixture to the skillet and stir until the sauce thickens.

Add the scallions, reduce the heat to low, and cook for 30 seconds. Remove the garlic, peppers, and ginger. *Serves 4.*

239 ▪ **Try using low-sodium Worcestershire sauce instead of soy sauce in recipes.** Robbie's low-sodium Worcestershire sauce contains 45 milligrams of sodium per tablespoon, compared to 1,000 milligrams of sodium per tablespoon of soy sauce. *One Salt Shaker.*

240 ▪ **If you enjoy the convenience of heating up a TV dinner from time to time,** look in health food stores for brands that are lower in salt (and healthier in other ways) than mainstream TV dinners. Shelton's Whole-Wheat Turkey Pie, for example, is made with whole-grain flour instead of refined white flour, sea salt instead of refined salt, no hydrogenated oils or preservatives, and 360 milligrams of sodium. It's not *low* in sodium, but it is 80 percent lower in sodium than the Stouffer's Turkey Pie, which has a hard-to-imagine 1,735 milligrams of sodium as well as hydrogenated oils and preservatives. *Three Salt Shakers.*

GO FISH

241 ▪ **Saltwater fish have only slightly more sodium than freshwater fish,** but both kinds are low in sodium. Whether you prefer saltwater cod or halibut, or freshwater trout or catfish, prepare fish with low-sodium ingredients and enjoy! *One Salt Shaker.*

242 ▪ **Buy fresh fish.** According to the *American Heart Association Low-Salt Cookbook*, frozen fish is usually frozen in salty brine. Besides, even if frozen fish isn't packed in a salty solution, fresh fish always tastes better. *One Salt Shaker.*

243 ▪ **Lemon-ize fish.** Freshly squeezed lemon juice is a natural for topping fish. Its tang complements fish so nicely that often no salt is needed. *One Salt Shaker.*

▪ BONUS TIP: *If you use freshly squeezed lemon juice regularly in your cooking, try this trick: squeeze 1¹/₂ cups at a time and pour the juice into an ice cube tray to freeze. This gives you instant fresh lemon juice cubes that you can add to cooked dishes and saves you from squeezing the juice fresh each and every time.*

244 ▪ **Brush fish lightly with melted Herb Butter or herbed oil (in tips 42 or 44).** Top with additional herbs like dill if desired, and bake until done. Fish cooked this way is so simple to prepare, yet so good. *One Salt Shaker.*

▪ BONUS TIP: *The time needed to cook fish will vary, depending on the thickness of the fish. As a general rule, ten minutes of baking is needed per inch of fish thickness.*

245 ▪ **Ground mustard powder has such a robust flavor** that it can eliminate the need for salt in recipes. Try adding ¹/₄ teaspoon of mustard powder to a marinade or baste for four people. Here's one simple example: ¹/₃ cup fresh lemon juice combined with ¹/₄ teaspoon dry mustard powder and ¹/₂ teaspoon tarragon leaves. Use to brush over fish before broiling. *One Salt Shaker.*

246 ▪ **Be sure to eat cold-water fish rich in Omega 3 essential fatty acids (EFAs)** —fish like salmon, mackerel, trout, haddock, and tuna. Omega 3 EFAs are protective for the heart and known to lower cholesterol and blood pressure. One low-

sodium entrée that's rich in Omega 3 EFAs as well as delicious
and easy to prepare is trout almondine. Make it by topping each
baked or broiled piece of trout with a drizzle of almond oil and a
few teaspoons of home-toasted slivered almonds. *One Salt Shaker.*

247 ▪ **Avoid breaded commercial fish fillets.** Not only are
they fried, but the breading used to coat them is also high in
salt. (Two Gorton's Breaded Fish Fillets, for example, contain
480 milligrams of sodium.) In this recipe from *Cooking for
Healthy Healing*, Linda Rector-Page has developed a healthier
"fried" fish that has a crunchy, nutty coating made out of sesame
seeds. *Two Salt Shakers.*

▪ SESAME FISH ▪

2 pounds 1-inch-thick white fish fillets, rinsed and cut
    into 6 serving pieces
Dash of black pepper and several sprinkles of sesame salt
Whole grain flour
$^1/_2$ cup whole grain bread crumbs
4 tablespoons pan-roasted sesame seeds
1 egg
2 tablespoons water or white wine
Olive oil

Lightly season fish pieces with pepper and sesame salt, then
dust them with whole grain flour. Combine the bread crumbs
and sesame seeds. Separately mix the egg and water or wine.
Dip the fish pieces in the egg mix, then in the crumb mixture to
coat well. Cover the bottom of a shallow baking dish with olive
oil. Lay the fish pieces in a single layer and bake at 350 degrees
for 10 minutes until the fish is firm and white. If you'd like a
simple, low-sodium sauce, mix together $^1/_4$ cup chopped fresh
parsley, $^1/_4$ cup lemon juice, and $^1/_2$ cup chopped green onions
and spoon it over the fish when serving. *Serves 6.*

248 ▪ **Keep down the sodium content of meals that contain shellfish** by preparing foods like shrimp and scallops with low-sodium ingredients. (Especially avoid using salted butter sauces or soy sauce.) Try tasty, low-sodium combinations such as herbed oil, lemon juice, and minced garlic; low-sodium tomato juice, onions, green peppers, and Italian seasonings; or Herb Butter (see tip 42) and white wine. *One to Two Salt Shakers.*

AMBER WAVES OF GRAINS AND BEANS

249 ▪ **Although it has become a favorite in much of America,** commercial white pasta is a poor food choice when you're getting the salt out of your diet. It is true that pasta is quite low in sodium, but it also is exceedingly low in most other minerals, especially minerals that balance sodium. When whole wheat grain is refined into white flour, 60 percent of its calcium, 77 percent of its potassium, and 84 percent of its magnesium are removed. Pasta made from white flour, therefore, is light on nutrition as well as being so bland that it almost requires salty sauces to give it some taste. Whole grain pasta, on the other hand, is more nutritious and has a unique, almost nutty flavor that stands well on its own.

▪ BONUS TIP: *It bears repeating that pasta is not the wonder food some lowfat diet gurus have made it out to be. Although pasta has been deemed a low-fat food that will help you keep the weight off, this idea recently has been refuted, even by notable publications like the* New York Times. *It's now known that high-carbohydrate meals like those centered around pasta cause the pancreas to secrete insulin, which is a* fat-storage hormone. *For an increasing number of people, eating too many carbohydrates like pasta can cause not only weight gain but also an increased risk of diabetes and heart disease. My books* Get the Sugar Out *and* Your Body Knows Best *cover this complex topic more thoroughly, but the most important thing to know is that it's best to eat whole grain pasta as a side dish with some protein instead of as a meal by itself.*

250 ▪ Skip sodium-rich Parmesan or Romano cheese on grains and pasta, and replace it with the flavorful, low-sodium combination of lemon zest and minced garlic. *One Salt Shaker.*

251 ▪ Use brown rice instead of white rice in your cooking. Brown rice is higher in minerals and has a chewy texture and delightful, almost nutty flavor that beats the blandness of white rice hands down. When my clients try brown rice, they find they simply don't have to butter and salt it, as they do white rice. To make brown rice, add 2 cups of salt-free vegetable, chicken, or beef stock and 1 cup of brown rice in a saucepan, heat it to a boil, then turn the heat down and let it simmer for 40 to 50 minutes (usually 40 minutes for short-grain and 50 minutes for long-grain). If you like, add some herb blends or a pinch of saffron to the cooking water for extra flavor. *Serves 4 to 6. One Salt Shaker.*

252 ▪ For a variation, make the same recipe using a combination of one cup of water combined with one cup of low-sodium tomato juice. *One Salt Shaker.*

253 ▪ If you live life in the fast lane, buy quick-cooking plain brown rice. Make it using a flavorful broth and season it to taste with herb and vegetable combinations or a teaspoon or two of reduced-sodium tamari (see tip 63) for a saltier flavor. *One to Two Salt Shakers.*

254 ▪ Avoid living life in the salty lane: stay away from instant flavored rice mixes like Rice-A-Roni. Half a cup of herb-and-butter-flavored Rice-A-Roni contains 790 milligrams of sodium and half a cup of its Spanish rice mix contains a whopping 1,090 milligrams. *One to Two Salt Shakers.*

255 ▪ **Combine brown rice with higher-sodium vegetables like spinach** to give the rice more of a salty flavor. That's precisely what nutritionist Melissa Diane Smith does in the flavorful recipe that follows. *One Salt Shaker.*

▪ GREEK-STYLE SPINACH AND BROWN RICE* ▪

1 cup short- or long-grain uncooked brown rice
2 cups homemade or low-sodium canned chicken broth
1 tablespoon extra-virgin olive oil
$^{1}/_{2}$ small to medium yellow onion, diced
2 to 4 cups chopped fresh spinach leaves (according to
    your preference)
Juice of 1 lemon or lemon juice to taste

Combine the brown rice in the broth in a medium pan and cook as directed in tip 251.

In a large saucepan or skillet, heat olive oil and sauté the diced onion for a few minutes until translucent. Then add the chopped spinach leaves and sauté just until wilted, about 1 minute. Add the spinach-onion mixture to the cooked brown rice along with the amount of lemon juice you desire and stir well. *Serves 4.*

256 ▪ **To make the above recipe slightly richer,** soak and drain one ounce of Greek feta cheese (as described in tip 197) and crumble it into the dish just before serving. *One Salt Shaker.*

257 ▪ **Try other grains such as barley, buckwheat, brown basmati rice, or wild rice in side dishes.** When you get the salt

---

* This recipe was adapted from a traditional Greek recipe handed down to Melissa from her mother, Helen Smith.

out, it's important to start putting other new flavors in. Whole grains add interesting variety to the diet, and if you prepare them without salt, you can rest assured that they're low in sodium but packed with other minerals we need. *One Salt Shaker.*

258 ▪ If you soak and cook dried beans from scratch, never add salt to the beans' soaking water. Don't add salt during cooking, either, until beans are tender: salt added beforehand toughens beans and prevents water absorption.

259 ▪ Add partially cooked beans to unsalted soups, casseroles, and sauces. Beans must be thoroughly cooked before you salt them or combine them with salt-containing ingredients.

260 ▪ Use hot spices to liven up bland beans. That's what the American Heart Association does in this recipe from its *Low-Salt Cookbook. One Salt Shaker.*

▪ VEGETARIAN CHILI ▪

1 cup dry kidney beans
3 tablespoons vegetable oil
2 cups chopped onions
2 cups chopped green bell peppers
2 garlic cloves, minced
1 cup no-salt-added canned tomatoes, chopped
1 cup bulgur wheat
1 1/2 tablespoons chili powder (or to taste)
1/4 teaspoon cayenne
1/2 teaspoon freshly ground pepper
2 tablespoons ground cumin
1 tablespoon fresh lemon juice

Soak the beans overnight in 3 cups of water. Drain the beans and place them in a large saucepan. Add 3 cups of fresh water and cook, uncovered, $1^1/_2$ hours, or until tender. Drain, rinse, and set aside.

In a large saucepan or Dutch oven, place the oil, onions, green bell peppers, and garlic. Sauté 8 to 10 minutes, or until the vegetables are soft. Add the tomatoes, 2 cups of water, and the bulgur. Simmer 45 to 60 minutes.

Add the cooked kidney beans and the remaining ingredients and cook an additional 10 minutes. Serve hot. *Serves 6.*

261 ▪ **For convenience when you're in a hurry,** use canned beans. Just be sure to discard the salty liquid in the can and rinse the beans well with water. Taking a couple of minutes to do these two things sends much of the refined salt down the drain. *One Salt Shaker.*

262 ▪ **Better yet, use very-low-sodium or salt-free canned beans.** Here are two brands worth noting: American Prairie, which makes organic canned beans that are low in sodium, and Eden, which makes organic canned beans that have no salt added. Both brands are available in natural food stores. *One Salt Shaker.*

▪ BONUS TIP: *Don't be afraid to add a few dashes of your own unrefined salt. It often helps with the digestion of beans.*

263 ▪ **Make refried beans at home without the salt** by mashing canned pinto beans with a broth, heating them, and adding spices of your choice like cayenne pepper, coriander, and cumin. Refried beans made this way are especially tasty when mashed with a flavorful broth such as the Garlic Broth in tip 167. Here's a dressed-up version of Refried Beans developed by Holly Sollars, a former demonstration chef from Canyon Ranch health resort. *One Salt Shaker.*

▪ ▪ ▪

▪ REFRIED BEANS ▪

$1/4$ onion, minced
$1/4$ cup green chiles, diced
1 garlic clove, minced
2 teaspoons fresh cilantro leaves, finely minced (optional)
$1/8$ teaspoon ground cumin
$1/2$ teaspoon dried oregano leaves
Mr. Spice Tangy Bang! sauce to taste (optional) [see tip
    289]
1 (15-ounce) can pinto beans, drained and rinsed (no-
    salt-added beans preferred)
$3/4$ cup Garlic Broth [see tip 167]
$1/2$ medium tomato, diced

Sauté all the ingredients except the beans, Garlic Broth, and
tomato for 4 to 5 minutes. Blend the beans and Garlic Broth
in a food processor or blender or mash them with a potato
masher, then add them to the sautéed vegetables. Add the
tomato, and cook for another 5 minutes. *Makes about 2 cups.*

VEGETABLES SIDE
AND CENTER

264 ▪ **Eat vegetables liberally each and every day.** Vegetables are high in potassium, antioxidants, and fiber and low
in sodium, sugars, fat, and calories. They also contain phyto-
chemicals—miraculous gifts from nature that help protect our
bodies against many diseases, including cancer and heart disease. No matter what research you review, it all says the same

thing: vegetables are just plain good for us. To ensure your best health, try to eat five vegetable servings daily. *One Salt Shaker.*

▪ BONUS TIP: *If you tried good-for-you greens like kale, mustard greens, or romaine lettuce but don't like their bitter taste, feel free to add a few dashes of unrefined salt to them. Salt appears to counteract bitter flavors, and just a small amount may make bitter foods like greens more palatable for normally staunch vegetable avoiders. It's much better to add salt to nutritious greens than to eat the salt hidden in processed foods. The high-potassium content of these valuable vegetables helps to counteract the sodium content in the salt. If a small amount of added salt helps you enjoy greens better, hopefully you'll eat more of them.*

265 ▪ **Vary the vegetables you eat** and use them in innovative ways to keep your diet interesting. (This is always important but especially when you're trying to cut down on salt.) In the following recipe from *The Yeast Connection Cookbook*, Marjorie Hurt Jones cleverly uses red pepper to form the flavorful base of a sauce for cauliflower. She developed the recipe for anyone who wants to avoid cauliflower in traditionally salty cheese sauce. *One Salt Shaker.*

▪ CAULIFLOWER IN RED PEPPER SAUCE ▪

2 cups chopped cauliflower florets
1 to 2 whole red peppers, chopped
2 to 3 teaspoons olive oil
Salt and pepper

Steam the cauliflower until done, about 10 minutes. While it's steaming, sauté the chopped red peppers in the olive oil. Use medium-low heat so the peppers soften instead of brown. Just before serving, use a blender or food processor to puree the pepper mixture into a beautiful red sauce. Add salt and pepper to taste and pour over the cauliflower. *Serves 4.*

266 ▪ **Choose fresh or frozen vegetables** over canned vegetables whenever possible. Although you can wash away much of the unnecessary sodium in canned vegetables, you can't restore the potassium that is eliminated during canning. (Canned vegetables lose at least one-third the potassium found in fresh vegetables.) *One Salt Shaker.*

267 ▪ **Avoid frozen vegetables that have seasonings or sauces added to them.** The main ingredient in most commercial seasonings and sauces is salt.

268 ▪ **Seek out frozen lima beans and peas that are labeled "no salt added,"** or use fresh or no-salt-added canned lima beans or peas. Before they are frozen, lima beans and peas are sorted by size in a bath of salted water, causing the vegetables to absorb additional salt. For this reason, regular, plain, frozen lima beans and peas always have more sodium than other plain frozen vegetables. *One Salt Shaker.*

269 ▪ **Steam vegetables instead of boiling them.** Steaming retains more of vegetables' crunchy textures and fresh flavors (in addition to more of the minerals found in raw vegetables). Boiling, on the other hand, causes vegetables to wilt and to develop "washed out" tastes that usually need much more salt for flavor. *One Salt Shaker.*

270 ▪ **Give piping hot vegetables an herbal touch:** lightly toss them with a few teaspoons of Herb Butter, herbed oil (see tips 42, 44), herbed vinegar, or any low-sodium herbal vinaigrette. Try cooked cabbage with Caraway Butter (see tip 137), baked tomato slices with garlic-marjoram herbed oil, or steamed brussels sprouts with dill vinaigrette. *One Salt Shaker.*

271 ▪ **Go nutty with vegetables:** make flavorful dishes like green beans almondine or broccoli à la walnut by oven-toasting slivered or chopped nuts until light golden brown and fragrant, then sprinkling them on top of cooked vegetables. Toasted nuts give vegetables abundant flavor all by themselves, but if you want a bolder nutty flavor, try adding a few splashes of unrefined almond oil or walnut oil along with the nuts. *One Salt Shaker.*

272 ▪ **Grill vegetables to give them a unique smoky flavor.** Simply preheat a grill or broiler and glaze your favorite vegetables with olive oil, canola oil, peanut oil, or sesame oil. (Eggplant and zucchini sliced lengthwise work particularly well.) Cook the vegetables for about 6 minutes, then turn them over and cook until tender. *One Salt Shaker.*

273 ▪ **Stir-sauté vegetables, with or without meat.** This method of cooking vegetables is a particularly popular one, and you can make stir-fries with different ethnic accents depending on the ingredients you use. Make Mediterranean-style vegetables by sautéing them in olive oil with garlic, oregano, and basil. *One Salt Shaker.*

274 ▪ **Change the stir-fry to Thai-style** by switching to peanut oil and adding seasonings such as garlic, chili powder, coriander, and lemongrass. *One Salt Shaker.*

275 ▪ **Or prepare vegetables Oriental-style** by using sesame oil, ginger, and garlic, as I have done in the following recipe. *One Salt Shaker.*

▪ **SESAME BROCCOLI AND CARROTS** ▪

2 cups broccoli florets
2 carrots, cut into rounds
$1^{1}/_{2}$ tablespoons sesame oil
$^{1}/_{2}$-inch piece fresh gingerroot, finely chopped
3 large garlic cloves, pressed
1 tablespoon sesame seeds
2 tablespoons sesame salt (optional) (see tip 58)

Steam the broccoli and carrots until almost tender, about 7 minutes. Heat the sesame oil in a frying pan and add the ginger, garlic, and sesame seeds. Cook, stirring continuously, until the sesame seeds are lightly toasted, about 1 or 2 minutes. Add the steamed vegetables and stir together with sesame salt. *Serves 4 to 6.*

276 ▪ **Satisfy your sweet tooth by using sweet spices on vegetables.** Cinnamon tastes great on baked carrots, and grated orange peel with ground nutmeg is a delicious combination on baked winter squash. One sweet spice combination I enjoy using in vegetable stir-fries is Chinese five-spice powder, a mixture sold in the Oriental foods section of supermarkets. This spice mixture makes you totally forget about salt; it gives vegetables a sweet, slightly licoricelike flavor. To use it, sauté a colorful assortment of chopped vegetables in half a cup of low-sodium vegetable broth or chicken broth, then add cooked brown rice and $1/4$ teaspoon Chinese five-spice powder to the mixture. Stir and serve. *One Salt Shaker.*

▪ BONUS TIP: *To make it easier to enjoy a wide variety of healthful vegetables when you don't have the time or energy to chop them, buy ready-to-use bags of pre-cut vegetable combinations. They are becoming increasingly available in the produce and frozen food sections of most supermarkets. If your local grocery store has a salad bar, you also can select chopped vegetables from there to use in stir-fries and other dishes. These two coping skills make meal preparation ultraquick and are lifesavers when you've had a particularly hard day.*

277 ▪ **Try sautéing vegetables in the Quick Herb Stock (see tip 164) or the Garlic Broth (see tip 167).** Either of these aromatic stocks will give vegetables plenty of flavor without salt or fat. *One Salt Shaker.*

278 ▪ **If you love tomato-based dishes like spaghetti and chili,** make salt-free tomato products staples in your kitchen. You can reduce salt in your diet dramatically just by switching from using regular canned tomato products to salt-free varieties.

Here's one example: use one 16-ounce can of unsalted chopped tomatoes and one 6-ounce can of unsalted tomato paste instead of the regular (salted) versions of these products in a recipe, and you cut the sodium in that one recipe alone by about 2,000 milligrams! *One Salt Shaker.*

279 ▪ **Bake corn on the cob** instead of boiling it in salted water. Roasting corn in its husk intensifies its flavor. *One Salt Shaker.*

▪ ROASTED CORN ON THE COB* ▪

4 ears corn on the cob, in the husk, with the silk removed
Freshly ground black pepper to taste
Chili powder, garlic powder, or onion powder to taste
    (optional)

Soak especially dry ears of corn in water for a few minutes before roasting. Bake unhusked ears of corn in a 350-degree oven for 30 minutes. Remove the husk and sprinkle with seasonings to taste. If desired, top each cob with a teaspoon of unsalted butter first, then add the seasonings. *Serves 4.*

280 ▪ **Baked potatoes are so low in sodium and high in potassium** that you can afford to add a few tablespoons of shredded cheese or a lightly salted tomato sauce for flavor if your taste buds desire. You certainly should feel free to enjoy baked potatoes the traditional way, too: with a tablespoon of sour cream and plenty of chopped chives. *One to Two Salt Shakers.*

281 ▪ **What do you use as a healthy substitute for greasy french fries loaded with salt and salty ketchup?** Oven-fried potatoes that are topped Canadian-style with tangy malt vine-

* This recipe was adapted from a recipe for Roasted Corn on the Cob that appeared in *Healing with Whole Foods* by Paul Pitchford.

gar. Here's a recipe that is a flavorful variation on that theme. It comes from the American Heart Association Low-Salt Cookbook. One Salt Shaker.

▪ OVEN-FRIED POTATOES WITH OREGANO ▪

3 medium baking potatoes
1 tablespoon olive oil
$^1/_2$ teaspoon freshly ground black pepper
1 teaspoon dried oregano
2 tablespoons malt vinegar

Preheat the oven to 400 degrees.

Scrub the potatoes thoroughly. Cut each potato lengthwise into 6 wedges. Place the wedges in a medium bowl and cover with cold water. Let stand 30 minutes. Drain and pat dry. Place the potatoes and oil in a medium bowl and toss to coat evenly. Place the potatoes on a baking sheet and sprinkle with the pepper and oregano.

Bake 45 to 50 minutes, or until the potatoes are tender. Remove from the oven and sprinkle with malt vinegar. *Serves 6.*

282 ▪ **If you'd like a saltier taste on fries,** buy a plastic spritzer bottle and spray baked potato wedges with a salty liquid like reduced-sodium tamari (see tip 63) or soy sauce or Bragg's Liquid Amino Acids. By squirting these condiments onto foods, you get a salty taste from every droplet, but you definitely use less and consume less salt than if you sprinkled these condiments from the bottle or by the spoonful. A plastic spritzer bottle is a cheap, handy tool that has plenty of uses, especially in low-salt cooking. Look for one in supermarkets or the gardening section of department stores. *Two Salt Shakers.*

283 ▪ **Be a garlic lover:** utilize this pungent, health-enhancing vegetable in every way imaginable. Whether you sauté garlic in a stir-fry, add it to broiled meat patties, or stew it a long time in a flavorful tomato sauce, garlic is the perfect antidote for salt-deprived taste buds. (We also know that it's the ideal antidote for combatting high blood pressure, high cholesterol, and weakened immunity!) For a new way of experiencing the irresistible taste and aroma of garlic, try roasting it. Roasted garlic develops a more mellow, slightly nutty flavor, and it's a great party pleaser. It's also simple to make, as this recipe demonstrates. *One Salt Shaker.*

▪ ROASTED GARLIC ▪

1 whole garlic bulb, unpeeled

Leave the garlic bulb intact and place it in a shallow baking dish. Bake at 300 degrees for 40 minutes, or until the garlic is tender. Remove the bulb from the oven when done and let it stand for a few minutes to cool slightly. Slice the bulb crosswise in half and let each dinner guest separate a clove from the bulb and squeeze the mushy garlic from its skin onto a piece of whole grain bread. The garlic can be spread with a knife as easily as butter. *Serves 8.*

▪ BONUS TIP: *Try using roasted garlic in other ways. Add a few cloves to soups or stews, or try it in mashed potatoes!*

284 ▪ **Use onions liberally:** like garlic, they make flavorful additions to just about any meal and are believed to have similar health benefits (including the ability to lower high blood pressure). Branch out and start experimenting with onion's flavorful relatives—scallions, chives, leeks, and shallots. Chopped chives and scallions (or green onions) not only garnish baked potatoes well, they also make tasteful additions to virtually any lettuce or grain salad or salad dressing. Although leeks and shallots are not as well known in this country as other members of the onion family, they, too, lend distinctive flavors to foods as an alternative to using salt. Try shallots or sliced leeks in soups and stews, or sauteed with other vegetables. *One Salt Shaker.*

A SAUCE FOR ALL SEASONS

285 ▪ **The Latin root of the word *sauce* is salt.** Knowing this, you probably aren't surprised that sauces are pretty much synonymous with salt. If you avoid commercial sauces altogether, you can take a major step toward reducing salt in your diet, but entrées without sauces sometimes can be dry and boring. This section will show you that delicious sauces can be made with little salt, and believe it or not, sometimes with no salt.

286 ▪ **Sugar and salt often go hand in hand in sauces.** When they're together, they often "cancel each other out," fooling your taste buds into believing you're not eating much of either. Processed foods are problematic for exactly this reason: they're high sources of sugar and salt, yet many people don't even realize it. Consequently, a good way to cut down your salt intake is to reduce your sugar intake. The Center for Science in the Public Interest has reported that when sugar is eliminated in foods, the amount of salt needed to satisfy taste drops dramatically. To help you avoid sugar (which, in turn, will help you cut down on salt), try to buy sauces that contain 5 grams of sugar or less per serving.

287 ▪ **Don't use salty sauces to "cover up" the taste of processed foods or poor-quality foods.** Sauces should only be used to accentuate the flavor of whole-food entrées and side dishes, not to mask foods you would rather not eat.

288 ▪ **Discover low-sodium sauces that don't contain refined salt, refined sugar, or preservatives.** Robbie's is one line to look for. This company not only makes low-sodium Worcestershire sauce (see tip 227), but other handy and flavorful condiments like garlic sauce and barbecue sauce. Ask for this quality brand in health food stores. *One Salt Shaker.*

289 ▪ **Even lower in sodium—in fact, sodium-free** —are the sauces under the Mr. Spice label. They are the most helpful condiments I know of for individuals who need to be on low-sodium diets. "Mr. Spice" himself, David Lang, is an herbalist who has been able to use his knowledge of herbs and natural foods to create sauces that have great flavor without any salt, sodium, refined sugar, MSG, or preservatives. In addition, except for his low-fat Thai Peanut Sauce, all of his sauces are fat-free. During the past several years, all nine varieties of Mr. Spice sauces have won Blue Ribbon Awards (ranking in the top ten of their respective categories) at the annual American Royal International Barbecue Sauce Contest. This means that judges in blind taste tests put Mr. Spice sauces at the top of their classes, ahead of countless other sauces that contained refined salt and other unwanted ingredients. Mr. Spice sauces can be found in most natural food and specialty stores and some supermarkets. They come in these tasty varieties: the original Tangy Bang!; Garlic Steak Sauce; Honey BBQ Sauce; Ginger Stir Fry Sauce; Thai Peanut Sauce; Honey Mustard Sauce; Sweet & Sour Sauce; Indian Curry Sauce; and Hot Wing! Sauce. *One Salt Shaker.*

290 ▪ **What makes tomato sauce the classic Italian pasta sauce?** Plenty of garlic, onions, and fresh herbs. The secret of good Italian sauces certainly isn't the refined salt that is predominant in commercial spaghetti sauces. (The salt content is so high in pasta sauces that a half cup of most commercial brands supplies almost one-quarter of our daily recommended sodium allowance.) Here's a low-sodium tomato sauce recipe that is *real* Italian. It was developed by my staff and works well on grains, whole grain pasta, or cooked vegetables. *One Salt Shaker.*

▪ CLASSIC ITALIAN TOMATO SAUCE ▪

1¹/₂ tablespoons olive oil
1¹/₂ medium onions, chopped
3 garlic cloves, minced
1¹/₂ pounds fresh tomatoes, peeled and chopped, *or*
    1 28-ounce can of no-salt-added crushed tomatoes
¹/₃ cup no-salt-added tomato paste
1 tablespoon red wine vinegar (optional)
1 cup water
1 bay leaf
¹/₂ teaspoon dried oregano leaves, *or* salt-free Italian
    seasoning
1 cup fresh basil leaves, chopped, *or* 1 tablespoon dried
    basil
3 tablespoons Italian flat-leaf parsley, minced (optional)
Black pepper to taste

In a heavy saucepan or stewing pot, heat the oil over low heat. Add the onions, then the garlic, and cook, stirring occasionally, for 10 minutes or until the onions are lightly browned. Add the tomatoes and tomato paste. Cook for 5 minutes and stir once. Add all the remaining ingredients, except the fresh basil and parsley, if using. (Note: if using dried basil, add it at this time.) Cover and simmer for 1 hour, stirring from time to time.

Add the fresh basil and parsley. Cover and simmer 10 minutes more, stirring once or twice. Remove the bay leaf. Let the sauce cool 25 minutes, then pour into containers. May be refrigerated for up to two weeks, or frozen. *Makes 4 cups.*

▪ BONUS TIP: *If you're using fresh tomatoes, the easiest way to peel them is this way: Make an X with a paring knife at the blossom end of each tomato. Core from the other end. Place the tomatoes in boiling water for 30 to 40 seconds. Remove them from the water and place in ice-cold water until they are cold to the touch. Pull the skin off each tomato.*

291 ▪ **Fragrant fresh basil** also forms the base of pesto, a versatile Italian sauce that is traditionally made with cheese. You can reduce pesto's sodium content significantly by cutting down on the cheese when you make it. In the following recipe, Holly Sollars uses herbed oil and a tablespoon of lemon juice to make up for the missing cheese in traditional pesto. The result is a reduced-sodium pesto that is still quite flavorful. *One Salt Shaker.*

▪ BASIL PESTO ▪

1^{1}/$_{3}$ ounces fresh basil leaves
2 garlic cloves, peeled
^{1}/$_{3}$ cup Spectrum Mediterranean Oil or other garlic
    herbed oil (or plain extra-virgin olive oil)
^{1}/$_{3}$ cup pine nuts or walnuts
2 tablespoons freshly grated Romano or Parmesan cheese
2 tablespoons water
1 tablespoon fresh lemon juice

Put all the ingredients into a blender and blend until smooth. Refrigerate for at least a few hours for best flavor. *Makes about 1 cup.*

292 ▪ **Combine small amounts of pungent condiments with salt-free ingredients** to create tangy low-sodium sauces. That's what Deliciously Simple author Harriet Roth does with mustard in the following recipe. *One Salt Shaker.*

▪ ONION-MUSTARD SAUCE ▪

1 large onion, thinly sliced and browned in 2 teaspoons
    extra-virgin olive oil
1 tablespoon coarse-grained mustard
Freshly ground black pepper
1¹/₄ cups salt-free chicken broth, defatted

Combine the browned onion with the mustard and pepper and
stir to blend. Add the chicken broth and bring to a boil. Reduce
the heat and simmer, uncovered, for about 10 minutes. Puree
the mixture in a blender or food processor, taste, and adjust the
seasonings. *Makes 2¹/₄ cups.*

293 ▪ **Make Instant Horseradish Sauce,** which is another
pungent example of a low-sodium sauté. It tastes great on
cooked meat, fish, or vegetables. Here's the ultra-simple recipe
I use. *One Salt Shaker.*

▪ INSTANT HORSERADISH SAUCE ▪

1 cup nonfat yogurt
1 tablespoon powdered horseradish (see Note)

Stir together and serve. *Makes 1 cup.*

NOTE: You can find powdered horseradish in fine gourmet
shops.

294 ▪ **Go Greek and cool as a cucumber.** Sometimes a
sauce that is refreshing and cooling is more appropriate than a
pungent or spicy hot sauce. Greek *Tzatziki* Sauce is one such
topper. It often is used to create a taste contrast for heavily
spiced beef, lamb, or chicken shish kebabs, but it also is a pleasant sauce on plain poached fish, too. This recipe is from my
book *Get the Sugar Out. One Salt Shaker.*

■ GREEK *TZATZIKI* SAUCE ■

$^1/_3$ cucumber, peeled, seeded, and diced
1 cup plain low-fat yogurt
1 garlic clove, minced, *or* 1 scallion, chopped
1 tablespoon fresh dill weed or $1^1/_2$ teaspoons dried dill
   weed, *or* 1 tablespoon fresh mint or $1^1/_2$ teaspoons
   dried mint

Combine all the ingredients in a bowl, cover, and chill for a few hours. *Makes about 1 cup.*

295 ■ **Don't be fooled into thinking a few tablespoons of a high-sodium sauce** like barbecue sauce couldn't hurt you. Commercial barbecue sauces contain exactly the kinds of sodium you should avoid, and some brands contain as much as 260 milligrams of sodium per tablespoon. That may not sound like a lot, but if you use three tablespoons of sauce on your chicken, you receive 780 milligrams of sodium—just from three spoonfuls of liquid! That many milligrams is almost the amount you would receive from eating half a day's worth of food on a low-salt diet. Make no mistake about it: all commercial barbecue sauces should be avoided.

296 ■ **If you really enjoy barbecue sauce,** don't give it up; just make your own. It's actually quite easy to do. And by making your own barbecue sauce, you can season it exactly to your taste and avoid the unhealthy refined salt and sugar found in commercial brands. Here's one basic recipe I like. *One to Two Salt Shakers.*

■ ■ ■

▪ ZESTY BARBECUE SAUCE ▪

1 (8-ounce) can no-salt-added tomato sauce
1 small onion, minced
2 to 3 garlic cloves, pressed
1 tablespoon low-sodium Worcestershire sauce (see tip 227)
1 teaspoon dry mustard
A dash or two of ground cayenne (optional)
2 tablespoons apple cider vinegar
2 tablespoons lemon juice
1 tablespoon blackstrap molasses, *or* apple juice
    concentrate
Real Salt (see tip 55) or Trocomare spicy herbal salt to
    taste (optional) (see tip 59)

Combine all the ingredients except the salt in a saucepan and heat over medium-high heat until the mixture boils. Cover, reduce the heat, and allow the sauce to simmer for 15 minutes, stirring occasionally. Taste and add Real Salt or spicy herbal salt to taste, if desired. Cool and refrigerate the sauce for future use. (Note: Both tomatoes and molasses can burn if heated too long. For best results when using this sauce, bake or grill plain chicken pieces and brush the sauce on the chicken during the last 5 minutes of cooking. A dab of extra sauce can be added after cooking if desired.) *Makes about 1¹/₃ cups.*

297 ▪ **Want something more simple?** Is opening up a bottle and spreading the sauce on more your style than cooking a barbecue sauce from scratch? If so, here's good news: Robbie's Barbecue Sauce, available in either mild or hot, is a convenient sauce that has no salt added, no MSG, and no preservatives. It contains only 15 milligrams of sodium per tablespoon. Mr. Spice's Honey BBQ Sauce, which also contains no salt, MSG, and preservatives, is sodium-free. *One Salt Shaker.*

CHAPTER 6

Get the Salt Out of Sandwiches and Snacks

Grain-based casual foods—such as pizza, nachos, and cheese crisps—are the second fastest-growing group of foods consumed in the United States, behind only snack foods such as pretzels, popcorn, and crackers. According to a 1994 U.S. Department of Agriculture survey, America's consumption of "grain-mixture" foods has increased 100 percent in the last twenty years, and its intake of snack foods has risen 200 percent. It's no coincidence that as our intake of processed carbohydrates like these has increased, Americans have gotten fatter. As I explained in the Bonus Tip to tip 249, too many carbohydrates, especially too many refined carbohydrates, can cause the pancreas to secrete excess insulin, and insulin is a fat storage hormone par excellence. But the refined salt content is as troublesome as the processed state of all the carbohydrates Americans eat. A typical serving of pizza (1/4 pie) easily can have 1,000 milligrams of sodium, and the sodium content of a sandwich—even what seems like a healthy sandwich with deli turkey slices on whole grain bread—sometimes can rival that amount. Add in a handful of pretzels for a snack, and with just those three foods alone, you often can exceed the maximum daily recommended amounts for sodium.

Make no mistake about it: typical varieties of casual foods, sandwiches, and snacks are laced with refined salt. If your diet is based on these foods, you're probably unknowingly consuming at least double the amount of sodium you should be. To change this unhealthy pattern, study this chapter well and get back to basics: eat three natural, square meals a day; munch on crunchy, fresh vegetables for snacks; and allow yourself fun foods like pizza as long as you prepare them in salt-smart ways.

The tips in this chapter will remind you just how important it is to eat healthful, satisfying, low-sodium snacks. Refer to this chapter often to reinforce the idea that salt does not need to come as part of the package just because a food is eaten by hand instead of with a fork and knife.

CASUAL FOODS

298 ▪ **To make quick and convenient pizza at home,** use the lowest-sodium, most wholesome ready-to-use ingredients possible. Mozzarella cheese, the traditional topping of choice, is one ingredient that meets these criteria; fortunately, it is one of the lowest-sodium cheeses available. Other ingredients to look for are Eden Pizza Sauce and any of the delicious, whole grain sourdough crusts made by French Meadow Bakery. You can find these helpful products in most natural food stores. *One to Two Salt Shakers.*

299 ▪ **Put plenty of flavorful, sliced vegetables on pizza** instead of pepperoni, ham, or Canadian bacon. This is a simple way to increase the potassium content and dramatically reduce the salt and sodium content of pizza. Tasty and colorful vegetables that can be used to top pizzas include: diced onions;

tomato slices; green, yellow, and red pepper rings; chopped spinach leaves; and sliced mushrooms. If you like canned artichoke hearts or sliced black olives on pizza, be sure to rinse them well with water before using. *One Salt Shaker.*

300 ▪ **Try pizza Hawaiian-style:** add unsweetened pineapple pieces to your pizza for a refreshing change of pace. *One Salt Shaker.*

301 ▪ **Use the herbs fennel and sage to create sausage flavor on pizza without the salt.** That's the creative idea nutritionist Melissa Diane Smith had when she came up with this recipe for a healthy Turkey Sausage Pizza. *Three Salt Shakers.*

▪ TURKEY SAUSAGE PIZZA ▪

TOPPING INGREDIENTS

1/4 pound lean ground turkey, crumbled into sausage-size
    bits (Shelton's brand preferred)
1/4 teaspoon *each* ground fennel seed and rubbed sage
1/2 teaspoon extra-virgin olive oil
1/4 small to medium onion, chopped
1/2 medium zucchini, cut in half lengthwise and sliced
    thin
1 garlic clove, minced

PIZZA INGREDIENTS

1/3 cup Eden Pizza Sauce *or* the lowest-sodium pizza
    sauce you can find
1 French Meadow Bakery whole grain pizza crust (see tip
    298)
1/2 cup part-skim mozzarella cheese (organic variety
    preferred)
Herbs such as dried oregano, fresh basil, fresh parsley, and
    more ground fennel and rubbed sage for garnish and
    extra flavor (optional)

To make the pizza topping: Heat a nonstick skillet over medium heat and cook the turkey crumbles for about 3 minutes, stirring often. Add the ground fennel and rubbed sage and continue cooking for about 2 minutes more, until the turkey bits are thoroughly browned. Scoop out the crumbled meat with a slotted spoon and place it onto a plate line with 2 sheets of paper towel. Lightly pat any unnecessary oil off the top of the meat with another paper towel, then set aside and allow the meat to cool. Clean out the skillet (drain away any excess grease). Heat the olive oil over medium heat, then add the onion. Sauté for a minute, then add the sliced zucchini and minced garlic and lightly sauté for 1 more minute. Turn the heat off and combine the cooked turkey crumbles with the sautéed vegetable mixture.

To assemble and cook the pizza: Preheat the oven to 375 degrees. Spread the pizza sauce evenly over the crust, leaving at least a $1/2$-inch rim around the crust that is unsauced. Spoon the vegetable-sausage mixture on top of the sauce. Top each pizza with $1/2$ cup shredded cheese, then sprinkle lightly with the suggested herbs or herbs of your choice to give the pizza extra color and flavor. Place the pizza directly on the center rack in the oven and bake about 15 minutes, until the cheese is melted and the crust is light brown. *Serves 4.*

302 ▪ **Make a cheeseless pizza.** It's a lot tastier than it sounds. Many of my lactose-intolerant or allergic clients who have had to eliminate cheese from their diets have told me that cheeseless pizza chock-full of flavorful vegetables and herbs often is as good as or sometimes better than the traditional kind. If you don't believe me, try following these instructions by Melissa Diane Smith for a cheeseless variation of her Turkey Sausage Pizza. *Two Salt Shakers.*

▪ CHEESELESS TURKEY SAUSAGE PIZZA ▪

TOPPING INGREDIENTS [see tip 301]

$^1/_2$ cup plus 3 tablespoons Eden Pizza Sauce

1 French Meadow Bakery spelt [a wheatlike grain] pizza
crust

$^1/_4$ teaspoon dried oregano leaves

$^1/_4$ teaspoon additional ground fennel and rubbed sage

1 tablespoon chopped fresh parsley leaves

1 tablespoon chopped fresh basil leaves

Preheat the oven to 375 degrees.

Follow the topping instructions as directed in the recipe above, but assemble the pizza slightly differently: Spoon 3 tablespoons of pizza sauce evenly on the pizza, leaving at least a $^1/_2$-inch rim around the crust that is unsauced. Then mix the $^1/_2$ cup of pizza sauce into the vegetable-sausage mixture and spoon the combined mixture evenly on top of the lightly sauced pizza crust. Sprinkle the recommended amounts of oregano, fennel, sage, fresh parsley, and fresh basil on top and place the pizza directly on the center rack in the oven. Bake for 15 to 17 minutes. *Serves 4.*

303 ▪ **Use salt-free seasoning packets when you make foods like tacos or fajitas.** (The Spice Hunter is one brand to look for.) If you aren't able to find a salt-free mix, season meat or poultry to taste with garlic powder, onion powder, and salt-free chili powder. *One Salt Shaker.*

304 ▪ **Make nachos and other similar snack foods with natural cheese instead of processed cheese products.** Natural cheese is salty, but it is lower in sodium than processed cheese. That means you should skip artificial cheeses such as Cheez Whiz and Velveeta and always opt for the "real stuff." Here's a recipe for homemade nachos that uses natural Monterey Jack. It comes from *Salt: The Brand Name Guide to Sodium Content* by the Center for Science in the Public Interest. They are a great improvement over the salty nachos offered at movie theaters, amusement parks, and ball games. *Two Salt Shakers.*

▪ NACHOS ▪

3 fresh corn tortillas, each cut into 8 wedges
¼ cup shredded Monterey Jack cheese
2 tablespoons chopped fresh green chiles, stems and seeds removed, *or* 1 canned whole green chile, rinsed and chopped

Preheat the oven to 400 degrees.

Lay the cut tortillas on a cookie sheet. Bake for 15 minutes, or until the tortillas are crisp and slightly browned. Remove the cookie sheet from the oven. Spread the cheese evenly over the tortillas, then spread the chiles over the cheese. Bake 3 to 4 minutes more, or until the cheese melts. *Serves 2.*

305 ▪ Hold the cheese on Mexican food to lower the sodium content further. Mexican favorites such as tostadas, enchiladas, and even tacos usually have such flavorful seasonings that they can be enjoyed without cheese. Here's a recipe for simple, cheeseless Bean Burros that have plenty of flavor. It's another low-salt idea from Holly Sollars. *Two Salt Shakers.*

▪ BEAN BURROS ▪

2 cups Refried Beans [see tip 263]
4 whole wheat tortillas (see Note, below)
Shredded green leaf lettuce, *or* half-shredded iceberg lettuce and half-shredded green leaf lettuce, for topping

Salsa [see tip 339], *or* other low-sodium salsa to taste (optional)

Heat the whole wheat tortillas in a 325-degree oven for a few minutes until warm. Divide the warm Refried Beans into 4 portions. Spoon each portion onto the center of each individual tortilla and wrap. Garnish the tops of the burros with shredded lettuce and salsa, if desired. *Serves 4.*

NOTE: The sodium content of whole wheat tortillas can vary considerably, depending on the brand. Garden of Eatin' is the lowest-sodium brand I know of; it contains 170 milligrams per tortilla.

306 ▪ Replace whole wheat tortillas in Mexican food with corn tortillas to cut the sodium even more. Whole wheat tortillas frequently average about 200 milligrams of sodium each, whereas corn tortillas usually are sodium-free and always have plenty of flavor. *One Salt Shaker.*

▪ BONUS TIP: *For a change of pace and color, try using blue corn tortillas. They, too, are sodium-free. Garden of Eatin' is one good brand you can find in health food stores.*

SANDWICH FIXINGS

307 ▪ High quality whole grain bread is delicious, but it can make your sandwich unusually high in hidden salt unless you choose bread carefully. One common whole grain bread I recently saw in a health food store contained 380 milligrams of sodium per slice! If you use two slices of a bread like that along with a couple of slices of deli meat, the sodium content of your sandwich can escalate to well over 1,000 milligrams. The bread that usually makes it into the sandwiches I prepare at home are any of the many varieties from French Meadow Bakery. Its spelt sourdough, which contains 55 milligrams of sodium per slice, is a personal favorite of mine. *One to Two Salt Shakers* (depending on the variety).

   ▪ BONUS TIP: *If you aren't yet familiar with spelt, you should be. It's a grain that is a close cousin of wheat and is loved as a gourmet food in many parts of Europe. Like wheat, spelt does contain gluten, but it seems to be more easily digestible and better tolerated than wheat (even by some who are allergic to wheat). Many of my clients who have given up white bread but are not yet used to the taste of whole wheat bread prefer the pleasant, almost nutty taste of spelt bread.*

   308 ▪ **A lower-sodium choice for sandwiches** is Garden of Eatin' Very-Low-Salt Bible Bread, a whole-wheat pita bread that contains only 30 milligrams of sodium per pocket. *One Salt Shaker.*

   309 ▪ **Or lower still is salt-free rye bread** made by both French Meadow Bakery and Rudolph's. If you're on a very-low-sodium diet, look for either of these brands in health food stores. *One Salt Shaker.*

   310 ▪ **Steer clear of cold cuts,** those convenient sandwich fillers that have the nasty habit of containing unwanted salt and sodium additives. (Even Healthy Choice Oven-Roasted Turkey Breast has 240 milligrams per slice!) Use instead:

   311 ▪ **Leftover home-roasted chicken, turkey, or beef slices.** *One Salt Shaker.*

   312 ▪ Or canned low-sodium tuna. Buying low-sodium tuna offers a substantial reduction in salt and a greater likelihood that if MSG is added, it will be added in much smaller quantities than it is in regular tuna. (However, buying low-sodium tuna does not guarantee that the tuna will be free of MSG.) Be sure to rinse even low-sodium tuna well. Fortunately, just one minute under the tap rinses away about 75 percent of the sodium. *One Salt Shaker.*

313 ▪ **Try hard-boiled egg slices on your sandwich** and add a potpourri of healthy vegetables like avocado and tomato slices, green pepper strips and spinach or dark lettuce leaves. *One Salt Shaker.*

314 ▪ **Spread your bread with unsalted peanut butter** or any other unsalted nut or seed butter of your choice. For a real treat, try thin slices of apple or pear on your sandwich in place of sugar-rich jelly. *One Salt Shaker.*

315 ▪ **If you buy deli meats** from a supermarket or deli that has its own oven, request "freshly cooked" turkey or roast beef slices. Some places will cook their own meat (which is much lower in sodium) if enough people ask for it. *One to Two Salt Shakers.*

316 ▪ **A healthy substitute for bacon, lettuce, and tomato sandwiches?** You bet. In the following recipe, natural-food recipe developer Holly Sollars makes an alternative for bacon with a soy food called tempeh (a vegetarian protein alternative that you can find in health food stores). You'll be amazed at what a close facsimile Holly's T.L.T. Sandwich is to the traditional B.L.T. *Three Salt Shakers.*

▪ ▪ ▪

• T.L.T. (TEMPEH, LETTUCE, AND TOMATO)
SANDWICH •

2 tablespoons Bragg's Liquid Amino Acids [see tip 64]. *or*
reduced-sodium tamari [see tip 63]
1 tablespoon light or dark sesame oil
2 teaspoons salt-free herbal blend (for excellent results,
use The Spice Hunter's Natural Mesquite Seasoning)
1 package soy-rice tempeh, cut into 18 slices (see Note,
below)
6 to 12 teaspoons low-sodium natural mayonnaise (1 to 2
teaspoons per sandwich) (optional)
12 slices French Meadow Bakery spelt sourdough bread,
lightly toasted, *or* other low-sodium, whole grain
bread
1 large ripe tomato, thinly sliced
12 red leaf lettuce leaves

In a shallow dish, combine 3 tablespoons of water, Bragg's Liquid Amino Acids or reduced-sodium tamari, sesame oil, and salt-free seasoning to make the marinade. Place the cut tempeh in the marinade for about 5 minutes.

Heat a nonstick skillet over medium heat arrange the tempeh in the skillet, and brown each side for 3 to 4 minutes, turning once. When the tempeh is cooked, place 3 slices on each sandwich.

Spread the mayonnaise on the bread, if using, and top with tomato slices, lettuce leaves, and a second piece of bread. *Makes 6 sandwiches.*

NOTE: Tempeh packages may vary. If you buy a package that contains 2 small pieces of tempeh rather than 1 large piece, cut each half into 12 slices and use 4 slices on each sandwich.

CONDIMENTS TO RELISH

317 ▪ **Carefully read the labels on condiments** and choose the ones that best meet your needs. If your diet is based mainly on natural foods, you probably can afford some salty seasonings, but be sure to choose brands that contain sea salt instead of those that contain refined salt. If your diet still contains too much salt (as most American diets do), buy the lowest-sodium condiments you can find. The best condiments that fit that description can be found in health food stores. They are:

318 ▪ **Spectrum Lite Canola Mayonnaise,** with 60 milligrams of sodium per tablespoon (compared to Hellman's or Best Foods, which both have 80 milligrams per tablespoon). *One Salt Shaker.*

319 ▪ **Westbrae Unsweetened Un-Ketchup,** with 60 milligrams of sodium per tablespoon. (This is a great improvement over Heinz, which contains 190 milligrams of sodium—over 300 percent more—per tablespoon.) Robbie's Ketchup is even lower in sodium, with 10 milligrams per tablespoon. *One Salt Shaker.*

320 ▪ **Any Mr. Spice sauce.** They are all sodium-free. (See tip 289.) *One Salt Shaker.*

321 ▪ **Westbrae Natural No-Salt-Added Stoneground Mustard or Kozlowski Farms Gourmet Mustard,** which are both sodium-free. (By comparison, French's Yellow Mustard and Grey Poupon Dijon Mustard contain 55 milligrams and 120 milligrams per tablespoon, respectively.) Mustard is so naturally pungent that many of my clients say they hardly notice any difference between salted and salt-free mustard. *One Salt Shaker.*

322 ▪ **Try a dab of cheese-free or low-sodium pesto sauce.** Melissa Diane Smith tells me this is her favorite condiment to use on turkey or grilled chicken sandwiches. Use the Basil Pesto in tip 291 or a ready-to-use brand, such as Rising Sun Farm. This company makes an entire line of low-sodium pesto sauces, including a Pesto for Garlic Lovers that is free of cheese and contains only 24 milligrams of sodium per tablespoon. Look for Rising Sun Farm in upscale markets or health food stores, or call 1-800-888-0795 to find a store near you that carries it. *One Salt Shaker.*

323 ▪ **Add a spoonful of Instant Horseradish Sauce** from tip 293 to any sandwich. This condiment is particularly tasty on roast beef on rye. *One Salt Shaker.*

324 ▪ **Make your sandwich Italian-style:** sprinkle it with oregano leaves and red wine vinegar and olive oil dressing. *One Salt Shaker.*

325 ▪ **Experiment with adding flavorful chopped herbs to sandwiches instead of salt.** One of my clients tells me she enjoys chopped fresh basil leaves and chopped chives on turkey sandwiches. *One Salt Shaker.*

326 ▪ **If you like pickles with your sandwich,** keep this fact in mind: dill pickles normally have 238 times more sodium than fresh cucumbers. They do, at least, unless you go out of your way to find an unsalted brand. One product to look for in natural food stores is Pickle Eater's Vinegar-free, No-Salt-Added Kosher Dills by New Morning (508-263-1201). They contain only 5 milligrams of sodium per serving. *One Salt Shaker.*

▪ ▪ ▪

THE SNACK CART

327 ▪ **Want something crunchy to munch on?** Remind yourself that typical snack foods like chips, pretzels, and crackers are not only processed carbohydrates high in salt, but they are also foods that tend to put on the pounds when eaten in excess. Satisfy your need for a crunchy snack by eating fresh vegetables, the kind of carbohydrates you should be snacking on. They're packed with abundant nutrients, fiber, and powerful compounds that protect health, and they're virtually sodium-free. You can munch on vegetables without guilt, knowing you're eating the very best snacks nature gave us. Eat them plain or try:

328 ▪ **Celery spread with unsalted nut butter** —a quick, crunchy treat. This is an especially good snack for those with hypertension. (See tip 200.) *One Salt Shaker.*

329 ▪ **Jicama Chips Olé,** a recipe that uses jicama, a naturally sweet, crisp, tuberlike vegetable. The following recipe comes from the *Arizona Heart Institute Foundation Cookbook: A Renaissance in Good Eating. One Salt Shaker.*

▪ JICAMA CHIPS OLÉ ▪

1 jicama (1^1/$_2$ pounds), peeled, quartered, and thinly
    sliced
^{1}/$_3$ cup fresh lemon juice
^{1}/$_2$ teaspoon salt-free chili powder
^{1}/$_2$ teaspoon ground red pepper

Marinate the jicama in the lemon juice for 1 hour. Arrange on a serving dish and sprinkle with the chili powder and red pepper. Serve immediately. *Serves 4.*

330 ▪ **Vegetable "chips" served with a low-salt, low-fat dip** such as Greek *Tzatziki* Sauce (see tip 294). Vary the vegetables you use as dippers and cut them into attractive shapes. All of the following work well: carrot, celery, jicama, or green pepper sticks; sliced mushrooms; cucumber rounds; zucchini or yellow squash wedges; blanched asparagus spears; and broccoli or cauliflower florets. *One Salt Shaker.*

331 ▪ **If you really enjoy grain-based snack foods like pretzels from time to time,** you may treat yourself to them occasionally. Just be sure to eat healthier, lower-salt versions, which you can find in health food stores. Look for brands that are made with whole grain flour instead of enriched (refined) flour and with sea salt instead of salt. (Also be sure to avoid any that contain partially hydrogenated oils.) *Two Salt Shakers.*

332 ▪ **Better yet, snack on unsalted pretzels** such as the organic whole wheat and 9-grain pretzels offered by Barbara's, another brand you can find in health food stores. If you don't like unsalted pretzels plain, try them with a little unsalted mustard. *One Salt Shaker.*

333 ▪ **Buy unsalted, air-popped popcorn,** or for fresher flavor, air-pop your own. Drizzle it with a little heart-healthy oil like unrefined flaxseed oil or canola oil, and experiment with salt-free seasonings to vary the flavor. To make popcorn savory, try sprinkling it with garlic powder, onion powder, herbs of your choice, or any salt-free vegetable seasoning. *One Salt Shaker.*

334 ▪ **To make your popcorn sweet,** add a few dashes of cinnamon. *One Salt Shaker.*

335 ▪ **To make it hot and spicy,** lightly sprinkle with curry powder, cayenne pepper, or salt-free chili powder. *One Salt Shaker.*

336 ▪ **To add a slightly salty taste,** shake on a few dashes of powdered kelp or dulse (see tips 60, 61). *Two Salt Shakers.*

337 ▪ **To give popcorn a buttery flavor,** sprinkle it with nutritional yeast, a powdered food supplement you can find in health food stores. *One Salt Shaker.*

338 ▪ Like commercial popcorn, standard corn tortilla chips can be incredibly salty. They also can be undesirably greasy. Try some of the new lines of tortilla chips that are baked, not fried, and that contain no oil at all. Many of these brands (Unsalted Baked Tostitos, for one) come in unsalted versions that are sodium-free. Some of my clients are pleased to find out that they don't need salt on chips; they just like the crunch. *One Salt Shaker.*

339 ▪ If unsalted chips are too plain for you, dip them in lively, low-sodium salsa. This is a great way to put extra salt-free flavor in your diet at the same time you get the health benefits of eating fresh vegetables. For a quick easy-to-make dip, try this simple salsa recipe from my book *Super Nutrition for Women. One Salt Shaker.*

▪ SIMPLE SOUTH-OF-THE-BORDER SALSA ▪

2 finely chopped medium tomatoes
$1/2$ cup chopped scallions
2 tablespoons fresh (or canned and well-rinsed) chopped
    green chiles *or* jalapeño peppers
1 tablespoon red wine vinegar

Combine all the ingredients in a bowl and chill in the refrigerator before serving. *Makes about 1 cup.*

340 ▪ Another tasty way to serve tortilla chips is with freshly made (warm) Refried Beans. (See tip 263.) *One Salt Shaker.*

341 ▪ Instead of pretzels, chips, or popcorn, nibble on unsalted nuts, nature's nutrient-rich snack foods. I find it a shame that during our country's fat-free craze, nuts are one of the foods that Americans have been told to avoid. Nuts are wonderful foods that can keep you going for hours. They're good sources of protein and healthy fats and rich in nutrients such as potassium and magnesium, in which Americans are often deficient. Nuts satiate the appetite so well that they are the ideal solution for some of my clients who devour entire bags of fat-free chips and still feel hungry. When those same clients snack on unsalted nuts instead of chips, they find they need just a few to be satisfied. I recommend nuts as heart-healthy snack foods that can be eaten in moderation. If you don't like nuts plain, buy unsalted, dry-roasted nuts in supermarkets. *One Salt Shaker.*

342 ▪ Better yet, toast raw nuts yourself at home. Nuts are absolutely scrumptious when you eat them warm right out of the oven; the toasting process intensifies their flavor so much that they really don't need salt. To make these simple, delicious snacks, spread shelled raw nuts of your choice on a cookie sheet and bake at 275 degrees for 5 to 15 minutes (depending on the size of the nuts). Allow the fragrant and lightly brown nuts to cool slightly before eating. Pecans, almonds, and cashews make particularly tasty toasted nuts. *One Salt Shaker.*

343 ▪ Don't be afraid to eat snacks that contain low-sodium protein. Especially if you're overweight, a slice or two of lean cooked meat or a hard-boiled egg may be the ideal snack for you. Protein like this increases the metabolism and causes the body to produce glucagon, a hormone that acts like a key to help the body burn fat stores for energy. Carbohydrates like pretzels and chips, on the other hand, cause the body to secrete insulin, a hormone that works in exactly the opposite way, helping to promote fat storage. Instead of eating processed carbohydrates for snacks, eat small amounts of protein. Natural, lean animal protein is lower in sodium than typical snack foods, and it also promotes weight loss better. *One Salt Shaker.*

CHAPTER 7

Get the Salt Out of Drinks and Party Foods

Beverages are so overlooked as important parts of our diets that many clients whom I ask to keep detailed food diaries fail to write down what they drink. Like most people, my clients seem to have a hard time remembering that although liquids seem insignificant, they really have a major impact on our nutritional status and health. Our thirst response is, after all, a call to satisfy the body's need for water. The body requires water for countless reasons, but often it is needed to be able to flush unnecessary sodium (and other minerals) out of the system.

Unfortunately, far too few of us drink the water we need. Most of the beverages Americans drink—although not high in sodium themselves—actually stress the body's sodium-balancing mechanisms. Caffeine-, sugar-, and alcohol-containing drinks indirectly hinder the body's ability to remove any unnecessary salt we may consume. In addition some drinks, such as vegetable juice cocktail, are quite high in salt, placing an additional burden on the body's sodium-regulating functions. The tips in this section address the importance of the drinks you consume. They'll help give you the savvy to avoid salty drinks as well as to eliminate those drinks that inhibit the body's ability to get the salt out.

Unlike beverages that we consume frequently throughout the day, party foods are meant for special occasions. Unfortunately, from what I have seen, parties in this country are often salt-filled events. Whether chips and dip are served, or smoked meat and cheese slices, or upscale hors d'oeuvres, it seems almost impossible to avoid consuming unhealthy levels of sodium at parties. Even normally health-conscious hosts often break their nutritional guidelines and serve refined salty foods at parties because somehow it's expected. The same often holds true during holidays. I find that hosts often feel pressured to serve overly salted foods for holiday meals, many times because of "tradition."

The tips in this chapter remind you that traditional festive foods can be vastly improved and needn't jeopardize your salt-cutting resolutions. Rely on this chapter to use abundantly fresh, flavorful ingredients in the party and holiday foods you prepare, and you can get the refined salt out of them without anyone even noticing.

DRINKING TO HEALTH

344 ▪ **Do not drink the following beverages:** added-sugar-rich fruit juices and soft drinks and caffeine-containing coffee and tea. Although none of these drinks are high in sodium, they all stress the adrenal glands and kidneys, organs that help the body metabolize and excrete sodium properly. An important way to get the unnecessary sodium out is to eliminate drinks that impede these organs' sodium-regulating functions.

345 ▪ **Avoid saccharin-sweetened diet drinks.** Although you may think saccharin tastes sweet, it is actually another form of *sodium* that contributes to our excessive sodium intake. In addition, saccharin in high doses has been shown to cause liver damage and cancer in test animals.

■ BONUS TIP: *Also steer clear of drinks sweetened with aspartame (NutraSweet). Five deaths and at least seventy different symptoms have been reported to result from the use of aspartame. For more information about the hazards of aspartame, see my book* Get the Sugar Out.

346 ■ **At parties, remember to order seltzer or low-sodium bottled water** instead of club soda. (See tips 120, 121, and 123.) *One Salt Shaker.*

347 ■ **Trying to get extra vegetables in your diet by drinking vegetable juice cocktail?** If so, you're probably doing your body more harm than good. Hidden in six ounces of V-8 juice—a drink that sounds so healthy—is 625 milligrams of sodium! It's better to add vegetables elsewhere in your diet and stick to drinking good, old-fashioned water, the beverage we were meant to drink.

348 ■ **What's the saltiest drink available?** Bloody Mary mix, a drink I have seen many men on airplane flights guzzle down as if it were water. If you thought Bloody Mary mix was a nice alternative to soda, learn the facts about how unhealthy this beverage really is: 8 ounces of Mr. & Mrs. T's Bloody Mary mix contains 1,350 milligrams of sodium and 8 ounces of Tabasco brand Blood Mary mix contains 1,550 milligrams of sodium. No matter whether you like Bloody Mary mix with or without alcohol, you simply shouldn't drink it.

349 ■ **You can, however, make your own.** Here's a healthy substitute that's great for parties. This recipe is courtesy of Mr. Spice (Lang Naturals). *One Salt Shaker.*

■ ■ ■

▪ THE WORLD'S BEST BLOODY MARY ▪

1 quart low-sodium tomato juice
2 tablespoons Mr. Spice Tangy Bang! hot sauce [see tip
   289]

Shake the tomato juice with the hot sauce. Pour into a tall glass over ice. If desired, add a piece of lime and vodka to taste. For decoration, you can also add a celery stick as a stirrer, if desired. *Serves 4.*

350 ▪ **Get into the habit of saying "no salt, please"** whenever you order a margarita (even if you order a virgin margarita). Salt around the rim of a margarita may be pretty, but it contributes up to 1,000 more milligrams of unhealthy sodium to each drink.

351 ▪ **The worst way to quench your thirst** if you eat too many salty snacks in a bar, for example, is to drink sugar-rich fruit juices, sodas, or alcoholic beverages. (Alcohol acts like sugar in the body.) According to Chinese food therapy, salty foods and sweet foods act in totally opposite ways: salty foods cause the body's fluids to contract while sweet foods cause the body to expand or relax. If you overindulge in salty foods, your body usually craves sweet drinks as a way to maintain balance. However, if you have sweet (or alcoholic) drinks, you then will want more salty snacks. A vicious cycle results—an unhealthy salt-sugar or salt-alcohol interdependence that is often hard to break. (Bar owners count on this cycle, frequently providing free, salt-soaked tidbits on every table to increase the sales of alcoholic drinks.) To prevent this unhealthy habit from beginning, simply try to avoid salty snacks at bars, nightclubs, and parties. If you do accidentally eat more salty snacks than you should, stop the cycle dead in its tracks: order low-sodium bottled water and drink plenty of it to flush the unnecessary salt out of your system. Evian is a good, low-sodium brand of water you can order in most places.

- BONUS TIP: *If you have high blood pressure, avoid alcohol as much as possible. Although it is low in sodium, alcohol contributes to hypertension, just like salt. Even if you don't have high blood pressure, much evidence suggests that you also should avoid drinking alcohol, except for occasional glasses of wine. Alcohol interferes with the utilization of essential fatty acids and can prematurely age the skin. In excess, it also can cause liver dysfunction, malnutrition, depression, and blood-sugar instability. However, research also shows that wine contains beneficial substances that may raise good HDL cholesterol levels and may protect against heart disease. If you do decide to drink wine occasionally, drink no more than a glass or two a day, and try to buy organic wine (wine made from organic grapes, which don't contain potentially harmful preservatives) whenever possible.*

TAKE A DIP

352 ▪ **Salsa is a party favorite,** but you could be offering your guests a salty food if you serve a store-bought brand. Make salsa yourself instead. Homemade salsa always tastes better than the commercial varieties, and it is so quick and simple to prepare that there's simply no excuse for not making your own. The recipe in tip 339 is so tasty you can serve it to guests, and it takes only about five minutes to prepare. *One Salt Shaker.*

353 ▪ **If you want to have store-bought salsa on hand** just in case guests stop by unannounced, look for salsas by Mollina's Finest or Enrico's in health food stores. Both brands are made with sea salt and contain between 30 and 40 milligrams per tablespoon. *Two Salt Shakers.*

354 ▪ **Here's a party pleaser: Spicy Bean Dip.** Serve it with unsalted toasted blue-corn tortilla wedges for a novel (and just plain fun!) presentation your guests will love. *Two Salt Shakers.*

▪ SPICY BEAN DIP* ▪

$1^1/_2$ cups Refried Beans [from tip 263] *or* 1 (15-ounce)
    can of no-salt-added refried beans
1 cup Simple South-of-the-Border Salsa [see tip 339] *or*
    other low-sodium salsa
2 ounces freshly grated cheddar or Monterey Jack cheese
$1/_4$ cup chopped cilantro (optional)

Combine the beans and salsa in a saucepan over medium heat and stir to blend well. Heat until hot, then stir in the grated cheese and cilantro. Reduce the heat to low and simmer 5 minutes to allow the flavors to blend. Serve warm. *Makes about $2^1/_2$ cups.*

355 ▪ **Another dip that can turn a get-together into a fiesta** is guacamole. Make it by mashing the inside of one avocado and combining the mashed avocado with ingredients like finely chopped tomato, onion, salt-free chili powder, and fresh lemon or lime juice to taste. An even easier way of preparing guacamole is to mash up an avocado and mix it with the amount of low-sodium salsa you desire. *One Salt Shaker.*

356 ▪ **To make ultra-quick dips when you don't have any time to spare,** use salt-free mixing packets like those from The Spice Hunter or the Canadian Herb and Spice Company (both

---

* This recipe was adapted from a recipe for Spicy Bean Dip that appeared in *Feed Your Soul* by George Fowler and Jeff Lehr.

can be found in health food stores). Combine these savory herbal combinations with nonfat yogurt and a tablespoon of light sour cream for simple yet tasty dips that are low in both fat and sodium. *One Salt Shaker.*

357 ▪ **A small amount of miso (see tip 65)** is excellent for giving bland bean dips a slightly salty, robust flavor. This simple bean dip recipe from my book *Super Nutrition for Menopause* gives you an easy example of how to use miso. *Two Salt Shakers.*

▪ WINTER BEAN PATÉ ▪

4 cups adzuki beans, cooked and drained
1 tablespoon light miso [see tip 65]
$1/4$ teaspoon cayenne
2 tablespoons rice vinegar
2 tablespoons extra-virgin olive oil
1 garlic clove, minced
1 teaspoon dried thyme
1 teaspoon dried oregano

Blend all the ingredients in a blender or food processor. Serve with whole grain tortillas or crackers. *Makes 4 cups.*

358 ▪ **Emphasize vegetables at parties.** It's one way to make sure you serve low-sodium, nutritious foods. Do not use vegetables only as crudités around the dip; use them as flavorful additions to the dip itself. Here's a healthy vegetable dip idea from *Cooking for Healthy Healing* by Linda Rector-Page. *One Salt Shaker.*

▪ ▪ ▪

▪ MEDITERRANEAN SPINACH DIP
FOR CRUDITÉS ▪

1 bunch fresh spinach, washed well and chopped
1 cup plain low-fat yogurt
1 green onion, chopped
$^1/_2$ teaspoon dill weed

Blend all the ingredients in a blender until finely chopped.
Makes 1$^1/_3$ cups.

359 ▪ **Use the rich flavor of unsalted nut butters** to create tasty dips. Sesame seed butter, known as tahini, is the most
popular nut butter used in dips. It's a standard in Middle Eastern hummus (a chickpea bean dip with garlic, olive oil, and
lemon) and Greek babaghanoush (eggplant pâté with garlic,
olive oil, and lemon). Other nut butters such as almond butter
also can be used creatively. In the following recipe, nutritionist
Melissa Diane Smith combines unsalted peanut butter with
yogurt, ginger, garlic, onion, and aromatic sweet spices to create
an exotic Thai Peanut Dip. *One Salt Shaker.*

▪ THAI PEANUT DIP ▪

1 small to medium onion, finely chopped
1 tablespoon sesame or peanut oil
1 to 2 garlic cloves, crushed
Small piece of fresh gingerroot, peeled and finely chopped
2 teaspoons ground coriander
Pinch of turmeric
$^3/_4$ teaspoon ground cumin (optional)
1 cup plain nonfat yogurt
1 cup unsalted and unsweetened natural-style peanut butter
Juice of 1 lemon
Chopped fresh parsley for garnish

Sauté the onion in the oil a few minutes until soft. Add the garlic and ginger to the onion and cook for another minute. Mix in the spices and the yogurt and cook over low heat for 10 to 15 minutes, until the mixture thickens and most of the liquid is absorbed. Combine the cooked yogurt mixture, peanut butter, and lemon juice in a blender or food processor and blend until the dip is medium-thick in consistency. Add a few drops of water or lemon juice if the mixture is too thick, then blend again. Sprinkle chopped parsley on top before serving. Spread thinly on low-salt, whole grain tortilla or pita wedges or serve with vegetable sticks. *Serves 6 to 8.*

APPETIZERS AND HORS D'OEUVRES

360 ▪ **Transform low-salt entrées into low-salt appetizers** by changing the way you present them. For example, make cocktail meatballs out of the Herbed Hamburgers recipe in tip 231 or the Mexican Turkey Burgers recipe in tip 232. Bake the meatballs in a 350-degree oven for 15 to 20 minutes until done, then serve them on a festive warmed plate. *One Salt Shaker.*

361 ▪ **Miniature-style casual foods also make great hors d'oeuvres.** Double or triple the Turkey Sausage Pizza recipe in either tip 301 or 302, and after baking, cut into bite-size squares. *Two to Three Salt Shakers.*

362 ▪ **Or make cocktail burritos** instead of the Bean Burros in tip 305. Cut whole wheat tortillas in quarters or sixths, add a dollop of refried beans to each portion, and wrap into mini-burritos. Hold each one together with a frilly cocktail toothpick if necessary. *Two Salt Shakers.*

363 ▪ **Mini–shish kebabs are versatile crowd pleasers.** They can be made with chicken, turkey, lamb, beef, shrimp, scallops, or even a firm fish like swordfish. To make them, marinate the pieces in a low-sodium salad dressing like herbal vinaigrette or a combination of lemon juice, herbed olive oil, garlic, and Italian seasonings. Skewer the marinated pieces on wooden sticks that have been soaked in water for at least 30 minutes, then broil. Add a few dashes of herbal salt if desired. *One to Two Salt Shakers.*

364 ▪ **Make festive broiled vegetable brochettes** to go alongside the meat kebabs. Colorful vegetables to arrange on skewers are zucchini and yellow squash rounds, bell pepper and onion chunks, and whole mushrooms and cherry tomatoes. *One Salt Shaker.*

365 ▪ **Dress up chicken drumsticks** by brushing with any Mr. Spice sauce before baking. (See tip 289.) *One Salt Shaker.*

366 ▪ **Or dress them up with flavorful herbs** that are beneficial to the mind and body. One herb, rosemary, for example, has for centuries been used as a folk remedy to combat stress and bring about positive effects on the mind. Some research suggests that rosemary does in fact lessen stress, presumably because of a compound it contains called rosemaricine or possibly because of its rich calcium content. Rosemary also is known to contain potent antioxidant substances. I tend to use this aromatic herb as a flavorful, healthy addition to fancy party foods. Here's a recipe from Jane Kinderlehrer, author of *Smart Chicken*, who uses rosemary to add a sophisticated touch to chicken leg appetizers. *One Salt Shaker.*

▪ ▪ ▪

▪ STUFFED BROILED CHICKEN LEGS
ROSEMARY ▪

8 whole chicken legs
1^1/$_2$ teaspoons sodium-free herbal seasoning
Pepper
1 tablespoon canola oil
^{1}/$_4$ cup lemon or lime juice
2 teaspoons dried rosemary
2 teaspoons prepared mustard
Parsley and 1 orange, in sections, for garnish

Carefully pull the skin of the thigh away from the meat. Sprinkle the flesh with herbal seasoning and pepper. Blend together the oil with the lemon or lime juice, rosemary, and mustard. Spread about 2 teaspoons of this mixture under the skin of each thigh. Place the chicken pieces, skin side down, in a broiling pan coated with nonstick cooking spray (or oil). Broil about 6 inches from the heat source for about 14 minutes, or until brown. Turn and broil the other side for another 14 minutes. To serve, spread the cooked chicken with any remaining rosemary mixture (which has not come in contact with the raw chicken), pour the pan juices over the chicken, and garnish the platter with parsley and orange sections. *Serves 8.*

367 ▪ Serve simple appetizers made out of small portions of fresh fruit to balance out any spicy or slightly salty foods you may serve. Try offering kiwi cups (halved kiwi fruit) served with miniature spoons, or apple slices. (To prevent them from browning, soak them in lemon juice.) Another idea is to make miniature fruit skewers by threading whole strawberries and chunks of fresh pineapple onto long party toothpicks. *One Salt Shaker.*

HOLIDAY FOODS

368 ▪ *Moderation* **is the key word to keep in mind during the holidays.** Taste the special foods of the season, but don't overindulge. Understand that standard holiday foods like mashed potatoes, stuffing, and gravy have a lot of salt hidden within them. If you decide you want a regular serving of mashed potatoes, try to skip the gravy and stuffing, or if you want a little bit of everything, compromise and allow yourself a very small dab of each.

369 ▪ Drink a large glass of low-sodium, filtered water before a holiday meal. It will help take the edge off your appetite (so you'll be less likely to load up on too many salty foods), and it will also help your body rid itself of any unnecessary salt you may eat.

370 ▪ To lower the sodium content of your typical holiday meal, revise your holiday recipes by following the tips in the Lower Sodium Cooking Substitutions section in Chapter 1. For example, if a holiday recipe calls for three tablespoons of butter, substitute unsalted butter instead. Making just this one change will lower the sodium content in a recipe by 360 milligrams.

▪ BONUS TIP: *Also be sure to increase the heart-healthy potassium and magnesium content in meals by substituting unrefined grain products in place of refined carbohydrates. The extra potassium and magnesium supplied by whole grains will be helpful if you accidentally eat more salt than you should.*

371 ▪ If serving ham is traditional for holiday meals at your house, see if you can start a new tradition. Garlic- and rosemary-studded roast leg of lamb or roast turkey breast rubbed with sage are wonderful holiday entrées that are much lower in salt. *One Salt Shaker.*

372 ▪ **Make homemade gravy** instead of relying on a salt-laden mix. Try this basic recipe from *Secrets of Salt-Free Cooking* by Jeanne Jones. If you like, experiment with adding herbs for extra flavor. *One Salt Shaker.*

▪ **UNSALTED CHICKEN OR TURKEY GRAVY** ▪

2 cups defatted chicken or turkey drippings
2 cups unsalted chicken or turkey stock
3 tablespoons arrowroot
$1/4$ cup cold water
1 tablespoon unsalted butter
2 tablespoons minced onion
1 cup thinly sliced fresh mushrooms
Freshly ground black pepper
Fresh lemon juice (optional)

Heat the defatted drippings and stock in a saucepan. Dissolve the arrowroot in the cold water and add to the saucepan. Cook slowly over medium heat, stirring occasionally, until the mixture thickens slightly.

While the gravy is cooking, heat the butter in a skillet and add the minced onion. Cook until the onion is tender, then add the sliced mushrooms. Continue cooking until the mushrooms are tender, then add to the gravy. Season to taste with pepper and a little fresh lemon juice, if desired. *Makes 2 to 3 cups.*

373 ▪ **Old-fashioned bread stuffing** is a high source of sodium because there is salt in the bread as well as in the dressing itself. One way to reduce the sodium content of stuffing is to used cooked grains like wheat berries, brown rice, or buckwheat groats in place of bread cubes. In the following recipe, oats are used to create a lower-sodium dressing that still tastes very much like traditional bread stuffing. *Two Salt Shakers*.

■ OATMEAL STUFFING* ■

2 cups rolled oats
2 eggs, lightly beaten
2 tablespoons oil
1 garlic clove, pressed
1/2 cup finely chopped onion
1/2 cup finely minced celery
Freshly ground pepper and Real Salt [see tip 55], *or*
        unrefined sea salt [see tip 54] to taste
2 tablespoons minced fresh parsley
1 teaspoon salt-free poultry seasoning
$^1/_2$ teaspoon dried sage, rubbed in your palms
2 cups (or more) homemade or low-sodium canned
        chicken broth

In a medium-size bowl, combine the oats and eggs. Stir together until the oats are coated with egg and set aside to soak for 5 minutes.

In a large skillet, heat the oil, then add the oats. Toast the oats in the oil and stir and toss often until they are golden brown and make clumps, looking almost like ground beef. Add the garlic, onion, celery, and seasonings. Cook slowly until the vegetables begin to soften, about 3 to 5 minutes. Add the chicken broth and simmer until the liquid is absorbed, about 5 minutes. The dressing should remain moist even when the liquid disappears. Add a little more broth or water if needed. Serve hot. *Serves 6.*

* This recipe was adapted from a recipe for Oatmeal Stuffing that appeared in *The Yeast Connection Cookbook* by William G. Crook, M.D., and Marjorie Hurt Jones, R.N.

374 ▪ **If you make stuffing from a mix,** I recommend that you use either Shelton's Cornbread Dressing Mix or Shelton's Whole Wheat Dressing Mix. Although neither one is low in sodium, both are made with sea salt and are much lower in sodium than commercial mixes such as Stove Top. Shelton stuffing mixes also don't contain the MSG and partially hydrogenated oils found in commercial brands. *Three Salt Shakers.*

375 ▪ **What's a delicious holiday food you don't have to feel guilty eating?** Roasted chestnuts, a low-sodium snack that's so good it's mentioned in Christmas carols. To roast chestnuts at home in your oven, follow these instructions from Harriet Roth's *Deliciously Low. One Salt Shaker.*

▪ CHESTNUTS ROASTED ON AN OPEN FIRE ▪
(Or in Your Oven)

1 pound raw chestnuts

Pick over the chestnuts and discard any that are soft or wormy. Cut an ✕ on the rounded side of each chestnut. Place them with the cut side up on a nonstick baking sheet. Preheat the oven to 425 degrees. Place the baking sheet in the oven and roast for 1 hour, or until done. Sprinkle with a few tablespoons of water every 15 or 20 minutes during cooking. The chestnuts will burst open when ready. Remove the outer shells and inner skins before eating. *Makes ¹/₂ pound roasted chestnuts.*

376 ▪ **If you like to give food gift packs to friends for the holidays,** carefully select the assortment of foods you send and diplomatically let others know that you would appreciate the same courtesy. There's nothing nicer than giving foods to celebrate the season, but foods often found in gift baskets include salted roasted nuts, summer sausage, smoked meats, smoked cheese, and processed cheese spreads. All of these are high sources of sodium—an overlooked fact that does not convey your wishes for a healthy and happy holiday season very well. Instead of sending baskets with these items, start a health-promoting holiday tradition by giving gift parcels that contain unsalted roasted nuts, small amounts of natural cheese, and plenty of fresh fruit.

CHAPTER 8

Get the Salt Out of Baked Goods, Desserts, and Treats

I have stressed throughout this book that if you eat natural foods, you will consume less sodium. Desserts are no exception to this rule. If you buy processed desserts (the kind that are designed to sit on grocery shelves for months), you're much more likely to consume more sodium than you should. Surprisingly, many of them are laced with salt. For example, instant pudding is alarmingly high in sodium, with more than 400 milligrams per half-cup. On the other hand, our most natural dessert—fresh fruit—is essentially sodium-free. In between these two extremes are many low-sodium desserts, but almost all desserts found in traditional supermarkets, whether low-sodium or not, should be avoided because they contain refined salt (as well as refined sugar, harmful fats, and chemicals).

Although you probably don't think of desserts like cookies and cakes as being sources of excess sodium, they are. When you consider that baking powder has 300 to 450 milligrams of sodium per teaspoon, that baking soda has 1,368 milligrams of sodium per teaspoon, and that salt contains 2,000 milligrams of sodium per teaspoon, it's easy to see how the sodium content of baked goods can add up quickly. In addition, commercial baked goods are made with potassium-depleted refined white flour instead of whole grain flour, so they almost always contain more sodium than potassium. As I mentioned in the Preface, our bodies are designed to thrive on foods that are low in sodium and high in potassium. The tips in this chapter will show you how to create healthy desserts that are rich in potassium, low in sodium, *and* low in sugar.

Admittedly, many desserts are not high in sodium. (More often, they're simply loaded with unhealthy sugar.) The following tips, however, should help you understand that even when you eat the sweetest of desserts, you still need to be aware of the sodium you consume.

NATURAL, LOW-SODIUM DESSERTS

377 ▪ **Treat yourself to fresh fruit.** Whether eaten plain as a snack or artfully presented with garnishes in crystal goblets, succulent fresh fruit is a dessert that's special in its own right. It's also rich in nutrients such as vitamin C, potassium, and carotenoids, which most of us are lacking, and it's always low in sodium. For all of these reasons, fresh fruit is our best dessert, the kind we should eat as a treat most often.

▪ BONUS TIP: *It's important to understand that fruit is a source of sugar, even though it's a natural source. Too much sugar, no matter what its source, can cause weight gain and other health problems, so don't go overboard: be sure to limit yourself to two or three portions of fruit each day. See my book* Get the Sugar Out *for further information on how to maintain a healthy intake of sugar.*

378 ▪ **Bake fruit and add flavorful, low-sodium ingredients** to create an elegant dessert. The following recipe does exactly that. It is one of my all-time favorites. *One Salt Shaker.*

▪ BAKED APPLE WITH WALNUTS, RAISINS, CINNAMON, AND NUTMEG* ▪

4 cooking apples, such as McIntosh or Granny Smith,
   cored and pared
1 tablespoon unsweetened apple juice
1 tablespoon chopped walnuts
1 tablespoon loose raisins
1 teaspoon ground cinnamon
$1/4$ teaspoon grated nutmeg

Preheat the oven to 350 degrees.

Place the apples and apple juice in the baking dish. Fill the centers of the apples with a mixture of chopped walnuts, raisins, cinnamon, and nutmeg. Cover and bake for 45 minutes. *Serves 4.*

379 ▪ **Get into the habit of using sweet starchy vegetables in desserts.** Vegetables such as sweet potatoes and winter squash are naturally sweet, high in fiber, and high in potassium, yet quite low in sodium. This means they are terrific ingredients to help you make low-sugar, low-sodium, extremely healthful desserts. Try baking acorn squash and adding a dab of butter, a few drops of real maple syrup, and a dash of cinnamon and nutmeg. Or bake a sweet potato, scoop out the inside, and mash it together with one banana, then sprinkle with toasted chopped pecans. *One Salt Shaker.*

380 ▪ **Learn to shop for healthful treats in natural food stores.** Although commercial cookies and other baked goods usually are not exceptionally high in sodium, they do contain unhealthy refined salt (and other dietary no-no's like partially hydrogenated oils, refined sugar, refined flour, and baking pow-

---

* This recipe was adapted from a recipe for Baked Apple with Raisins, Cinnamon, and Nutmeg from my book *Beyond Pritikin*.

der made with aluminum). Health food stores sell goodies that are better on all these fronts: the desserts that are usually sold are made with sea salt, higher quality fats, fruit sweeteners or other natural sugars, and nonaluminum baking powder. Here's a good example: two Nature's Warehouse Whole Wheat Fig Newtons (cookies you can find in health food stores) contain only 40 milligrams of sodium, and they're made with figs, whole wheat flour, fruit juice concentrates, nonhydrogenated canola oil, baking soda, and sea salt. By comparison, two Nabisco Fig Newtons contain 120 milligrams of sodium, and they're made with enriched (refined) flour, preserved figs, three types of refined sugar, refined salt, corn flour, whey, baking soda, and artificial flavors. Always look for desserts that contain sea salt instead of table salt and that have the most natural ingredients you can find. *One to Two Salt Shakers.*

   381 ▪ Skip the instant chocolate pudding. Hidden in quick-fix pudding mixes is a hard-to-believe amount of salt: one serving of Jell-O Instant Chocolate Pudding Mix contains 410 milligrams of sodium, and a serving size of SnackWell's Instant Double Fudge Pudding Mix contains 440 milligrams of sodium. (What is so much salt doing in sweet pudding anyway?) If you occasionally like to treat yourself to pudding—and you want to make it in a jiffy—try this simple, wholesome pudding my staff helped me devise for this book. Not only does this recipe not contain the salt found in instant pudding mixes, but it also avoids other harmful ingredients often found in mixes—artificial flavors, artificial colors, and preservatives. *One Salt Shaker.*

▪ ▪ ▪

▪ QUICK CHOCOLATE PUDDING ▪

2 cups nonfat milk
1/4 cup Sucanat (dehydrated cane juice crystals, available
   in health food stores)
3 tablespoons unsweetened cocoa powder
3 tablespoons arrowroot
1 teaspoon natural vanilla extract
4 tablespoons lightly toasted slivered almonds (optional)

Blend the milk, Sucanat, cocoa powder, and arrowroot in a
blender. When the ingredients are well blended, pour the mixture into a medium saucepan. Heat on high, stirring constantly,
to prevent the milk from scalding. When the mixture begins to
thicken, turn the heat to medium and heat, still stirring constantly, until the mixture thickens to the consistency of a pudding. Mix in the vanilla extract, then pour into 4 pudding dishes
and allow to cool for 10 minutes. Cover and refrigerate for several hours. If desired, top with the almonds before serving.
Serves 4.

382 ▪ **To help your body get the salt out, get the sugar
out as much as possible.** According to nutritional expert
Melvyn R. Werbach, M.D., sugar inhibits the body's ability to
clear excess sodium and water. This results in water retention,
weight gain, abdominal bloating, and swelling of the face and
extremities. Even low-sodium desserts such as ice cream, which
is rich in sugar, should be avoided.

▪ BONUS TIP: *If you need more incentive to get the sugar
out of your diet, you should know that excessive sugar intake is linked
to obesity, heart disease, cancer, osteoporosis, and more than sixty
other ailments. My book* Get the Sugar Out *explains in great detail
sugar's relationship to disease, and it also has lower-sugar recipes and
501 tips that will help you cut your sugar intake.*

TIPS FOR LOW-SODIUM BAKING

383 ▪ **Change the sodium-to-potassium ratio in baked goods** to a ratio that is closer to what we receive in natural foods. Even if you use sodium-rich baking powder and baking soda, you still can improve the sodium-to-potassium ratio by increasing the potassium content of baked goods: use whole grain flour instead of commercial refined flour and add other potassium-rich natural foods such as fruit, vegetables, nuts, and seeds. Employing any of the following tips will also improve the important ratio of these minerals.

384 ▪ **Use unrefined sea salt or Real Salt** instead of common table salt in recipes, and try reducing the salt slightly. Usually a 25 percent (or even 50 percent) reduction in the salt indicated doesn't affect the quality of baked goods.

385 ▪ **When you double a sweet recipe, don't increase the salt;** it's not necessary. Other ways to reduce the sodium content in baked goods include replacing any of the following ingredients with their lower-sodium alternatives:

386 ▪ **Melted butter or margarine:** canola oil or melted unsalted butter. *One Salt Shaker.*

387 ▪ **Peanut butter, almond butter, or other nut butters:** unsalted peanut butter, unsalted almond butter, or other unsalted nut butters. *One Salt Shaker.*

388 ▪ **Buttermilk:** nonfat yogurt combined with nonfat milk. To replace one cup of buttermilk in a recipe, use $3/4$ cup nonfat yogurt mixed together with $1/4$ cup nonfat milk. This substitution provides 170 milligrams of sodium compared to 257 milligrams in one cup of buttermilk. *Two Salt Shakers.*

389 ▪ **A substitute for buttermilk even lower in sodium:** soured milk. To sour milk, add one tablespoon of brown rice vinegar or lemon juice to one cup of nonfat milk and let stand until it curdles. *One Salt Shaker.*

390 ▪ **Baking powder:** Featherweight Baking Powder. This product, which is available in many supermarkets, not only helps you get the sodium out, but it also helps you avoid the aluminum common in many baking powders. *One Salt Shaker.*

391 ▪ **Skip sodium-rich baking powder, baking soda, and salt altogether,** and use the natural leavening power of egg whites in desserts. Angel food cake and macaroons, which both contain egg whites, are two good examples of desserts that simply don't need traditional sodium-rich leavening agents. Macaroons are usually thought of as being made only from coconut, but they don't have to be. In the following recipe, ground blanched almonds are used to make a deliciously different kind—nutrient-packed Almond Macaroons. *One Salt Shaker.*

▪ ALMOND MACAROONS* ▪

3 egg whites
1 tablespoon natural almond extract
3 tablespoons Sucanat (dehydrated cane juice crystals, available in health food stores)
1 cup ground blanched almonds
21 whole almonds

Blanch the almonds in hot water to cover, remove the skins, and grind to a fine meal. Mix together the egg whites, almond extract, and Sucanat and add to the almond meal. Mix until well blended, then chill the dough for 1 hour.

Drop heaping teaspoonfuls onto an oiled cookie sheet, press a whole almond into the top of each cookie, and bake at 350

---

* This recipe was adapted by Melissa Diane Smith from a recipe for Lemony Almond Macaroon Drops that appeared in my book *Get the Sugar Out.*

degrees until light brown, about 5 minutes. The cookies will harden more as they cool. *Makes approximately 20 cookies.*

392 ▪ If you add raisins or other dried fruits to baked desserts, be sure to avoid those fruits preserved with sodium bisulfite, another form of unhealthy sodium in our diets. This preservative adds to our sodium load and is a common allergen that can cause health-threatening reactions in many people. Look in natural food stores for dried fruits that aren't treated with sulfites.

▪ BONUS TIP: *Feel free to add chopped nuts to cookies and cakes. Nuts are sugar-free and virtually sodium-free, and they supply protein and high-quality fats that slow down the quick release of sugar from sweets into the bloodstream. They also are packed with minerals like potassium and magnesium, which most of our diets are lacking. For all of these reasons, I find nuts healthful, flavorful, and extremely satisfying ingredients to add to baked goods.*

393 ▪ The main source of sodium in pies is the salt in the crust. (Fruit pies, for example, have extremely low-sodium fillings.) Fortunately, the salt in recipes for piecrust usually can be reduced and sometimes can be skipped altogether. In the following recipe from *Secrets of Salt-Free Cooking*, Jeanne Jones has created a piecrust recipe that uses cider vinegar in place of salt. If you're extremely sensitive to salt—or if you have a recipe for pie filling that's slightly salty (such as cheesecake filling)—use this Perfect Salt-Free Piecrust. *One Salt Shaker.*

▪ ▪ ▪

▪ **PERFECT SALT-FREE PIECRUST** ▪

1 cup whole wheat pastry flour
$1/4$ cup oil
3 tablespoons ice water
$1/4$ teaspoon cider vinegar

Preheat the oven to 375 degrees.

Put the flour into a 9-inch pie pan. Measure the oil in a large measuring cup, add the ice water and vinegar, and mix well, using a fork. Slowly add the liquid to the flour in the pie pan, mixing it with the fork. Continue mixing until all the ingredients are well blended. Press into shape with your fingers, making sure the crust covers the entire inner surface of the pan evenly. If the recipe calls for a prebaked crust, prick the bottom of the crust with a fork in several places and bake for 20 to 25 minutes, or until golden brown. *Makes one 9-inch piecrust.*

394 ▪ **Another way to get the salt out is to eliminate the crust altogether:** make a fresh fruit crisp or fruit crumble instead. *One Salt Shaker.*

CHAPTER 9

Get the Salt Out
When You Eat Out

Once you understand how and why you should get the salt out of your diet, it's fairly simple to avoid refined salt and sodium additives in the foods you eat at home. It's another matter, however, when you eat out.

When you dine in a restaurant, you no longer oversee every ingredient used in the preparation of your meal. That's part of the fun of eating out, but it's also part of the problem. In exchange for the pleasure of having other people prepare food for you, you put yourself at the mercy of the chef. Even when cooks don't add salt themselves, they often use commercially prepared foods that contain unwanted salt as well as sodium-rich flavor enhancers, preservatives, and additives. Excess sodium commonly sneaks into restaurant food this way.

If you are not careful, hidden sodium in restaurant food can sabotage the efforts you've made to cut the salt elsewhere in your diet (especially if you eat out often). Prevent this from happening by becoming as knowledgeable and selective about the meals you order in restaurants as you are about the products you buy in grocery stores. You already have a solid foundation for getting the salt out when you eat out: all the salt-cutting skills you've learned in the other chapters can easily be applied to dining in restaurants. The tips in this chapter build on that foundation, teaching you the all-important skills of being a salt-smart diner and traveler.

GETTING WHAT YOU WANT

395 ▪ **Patronize restaurants where food is cooked to order,** and request that your meal be simply prepared—baked, broiled, or grilled—without salt or seasoning salts. *One Salt Shaker.*

396 ▪ **Also ask that your entrée be served without sauces or gravies** —or ask for them on the side and use them sparingly. *One to Two Salt Shakers.*

397 ▪ **To prevent bland food from arriving at your table,** tell the server that you'd prefer herbs to be used liberally in your order. *One Salt Shaker.*

398 ▪ **Or ask if chopped chives or other fresh herbs can be served on the side with your meal.** If you see on the menu that fresh herbs are listed as seasonings or garnishes in other entrées, this request almost always can be granted. *One Salt Shaker.*

399 ▪ **Ask for lemon wedges with your entrée.** Lemon juice always gives salt-free food more kick. *One Salt Shaker.*

400 ▪ **Pick and choose from the menu.** If a particular item appears somewhere on the menu, you should be able to get it with whatever entrée you want. If you see a romaine lettuce salad topped with teriyaki chicken strips on the menu and you also see a plain grilled chicken breast sandwich, there's no reason you should not be able to combine the lower-sodium components of both entrées and get a romaine lettuce salad topped with plain grilled chicken strips. *One Salt Shaker.*

▪ BONUS TIP: *Be bold yet polite when asking your server for special favors. If you have a hard time doing this, remember that you're the customer and it's in the restaurant's best interests to have a satisfied one. After your meal, reward your server accordingly: if he or she worked especially hard to accommodate your wishes, express your thanks to that person and be especially generous with your tip.*

401 ▪ **Consider carrying a small salt-free herb shaker to the restaurant with you.** (It's easy to carry a shaker to the restaurant in a purse or coat pocket.) If you're used to using salt-free blends at home, you'll probably enjoy low-salt foods in restaurants much more if you can season them to taste with your favorite herbal blend. *One Salt Shaker.*

402 ▪ **Carry "good" salt with you.** As I've mentioned throughout this book, the kind of salt you use is extremely important to your health. If you are careful to ask that your meals in restaurants be prepared without salt (which is always the refined variety), then adding a few shakes of natural salt is hardly ever a problem and, many times, can even enhance your health. (As I mentioned in the Preface, for many of my clients, especially those who have low-sodium blood levels, they actually need a little bit of natural salt added to unprocessed foods to achieve their best health.) Some herbal salts such as Bioforce's Herbamare and Trocomare (mentioned in tip 59) are available in 3.2-ounce shaker bottles that can be carried like salt-free herb shakers in a purse or coat pocket. The most helpful traveling salt shaker I know of, however, is an ultra-small, refillable, plastic shaker available from Real Salt. (See tip 55.) With dimensions of $1^1/_2$ inches by 2 inches by $^1/_2$ inch, this salt shaker can be carried anywhere because it can easily fit into any pocket. I myself carry one with me wherever I go, and I recommend this handy shaker full of healthy salt to all of my clients. See the Resources section for information on how you can order this convenient product. *Two Salt Shakers.*

403 ▪ Seek out natural food restaurants. By now, you probably know the rule: the more natural the foods are that you eat, the better. When you eat at natural food restaurants, you automatically know that the selections offered are made with fresh, natural ingredients and that the use of prepackaged or processed foods is minimal. Consequently, hidden salt in the food isn't as much of a problem. (Don't let down your guard though: even when you eat in natural food restaurants, you still need to be savvy about salt.)

▪ BONUS TIP: *An unexpected bonus on the tables of some natural food restaurants is shakers of herbal blends or healthy salt like sesame salt instead of common table salt.*

MENU SAVVY

404 ▪ "Heart-healthy" symbols on a menu *can* signal entrées that are lower in salt and sodium than other entrées, but not always. At one spa-type restaurant I visited, I was surprised to see a chicken teriyaki dinner labeled heart-smart: it may have been lower in fat and cholesterol than traditional fare, but it certainly wasn't low in sodium. (Just two tablespoons of teriyaki sauce contain about 1,300 milligrams of sodium!) The truth is that heart-healthy labeling on restaurant menus often is not regulated. Many restaurants put heart-smart symbols on their menus without American Heart Association approval or without even claiming that those meals are low in salt. If you visit a restaurant where heart-healthy symbols are used on the menu, don't consider the symbols rubber stamps that the entrées are good choices to order: judge for yourself whether each entrée sounds as if it is low in sodium, and also be sure that the entrée is not prepared with unhealthy margarine or excessive sweeteners.

405 ▪ **Get the salt out of breakfast** by avoiding surprisingly high-sodium croissants, pastries, and other baked goods, and all breakfast meats such as sausage, bacon, and ham. (These are sources of potentially carcinogenic sodium nitrites and nitrates.) Your best bets for breakfast are unsalted poached, scrambled, soft-boiled, or hard-boiled eggs; plain or vegetable omelettes without added salt; basic cereals such as oatmeal or shredded wheat; or fresh fruit. *One Salt Shaker.*

406 ▪ **Order salad as a first course instead of soup.** Just like commercial canned soups sold in supermarkets, the soups that are served in restaurants are overly salty because they're designed to satisfy taste buds used to too much salt. Until the public learns to prefer less salt in all its food, the best choice for a meal starter in restaurants will always be a salad. *One Salt Shaker.*

407 ▪ **The safest salad dressing to order** as far as salt and sodium is concerned is vinegar and oil or lemon wedges and oil. *One Salt Shaker.*

408 ▪ **If you must order a different salad dressing,** order it on the side and dip your fork into the dressing before taking bites of salad. *Two Salt Shakers.*

409 ▪ **Or put a teaspoon of the dressing on your salad and thin it out** with lemon juice or vinegar. Either of these options, however, isn't as healthy for you as oil and plain vinegar or lemon juice because most commercial salad dressings contain not only unhealthy salt but also undesirable MSG and hydrogenated oils. *Two Salt Shakers.*

410 ▪ **Better yet, bring a low-sodium dressing to the restaurant with you.** Two-ounce watertight Tupperware containers known as Midgets are extremely helpful for this purpose, enabling you to unobtrusively carry homemade dressings or unrefined oils with you just about anywhere you go. *One Salt Shaker.*

411 ▪ **Avoid ordering entrées that contain any of the following red-flag words or phrases:** soy sauce, tamari sauce, or shoyu sauce—three ingredients that should always alert you to a meal with a high-sodium content. Other ingredients to beware of are:

412 ▪ **Teriyaki sauce** (which is a blend of soy sauce, rice wine, and sugar).

413 ▪ **Barbecue sauce.**

414 ▪ **Breaded or battered entrées.**

415 ▪ **Butter sauces, cheese sauces, gravies, or *au jus*.**

416 ▪ **If you unknowingly order an entrée that comes with breading, topping, or a salty sauce,** scrape away as much of it as possible before eating. This coping strategy is particularly helpful when you're in a social situation in which it would be awkward to send the entrée back.

417 ▪ **What are the best side dishes to order?** A double order of steamed vegetables—or a salad and a baked potato—with toppings on the side. *One Salt Shaker.*

418 ▪ **To season a potato or vegetables,** you can use butter or sour cream, but try to limit yourself to one teaspoon of either. Even if you use salted butter (the kind which is usually served in restaurants), limiting yourself to one teaspoon will hold down the salt (and fat) content of the meal considerably. *One to Two Salt Shakers.*

▪ BONUS TIP: *If you do use salted butter in a restaurant, refrain from adding any extra salt at the table.*

419 ▪ **When you eat in restaurants, it's up to you** to avoid foods that commonly contain hidden MSG and excessive salt. Many restaurant workers may tell you that an entrée doesn't contain MSG or salt, but they often are unaware that packaged products used in the preparation of that food are laced with these two sources of unhealthy sodium. A good rule of thumb is to avoid eating restaurant food made from the same high-sodium ingredients that you would avoid buying in supermarkets.

420 ▪ Order fruit for dessert. (This choice is free not only of refined salt but also of refined sugar, too!) A goblet of berries always makes an elegant finish to dinner, and so do melon slices or fruit cocktail. Even if you don't see fruit on the menu, do not hesitate to ask for it. Most good restaurants have fruit in the kitchen and are more than willing to serve it to you. *One Salt Shaker.*

421 ▪ No matter how careful you are when you eat in restaurants, expect that you probably will consume a little more sodium than you do at home. If you understand this, you can prepare for it: when you know you're going to go out for dinner, eat as many low-sodium natural foods as you can the rest of the day to protect yourself from the excess sodium you may receive in that one meal. This coping strategy also should help you keep your sodium intake for the day underneath the maximum 2,400 milligrams.

INTERNATIONAL INSIGHTS

422 ▪ To add healthy variety to your diet, eat at ethnic restaurants as long as you are smart about salt when you do. First, choose the least commercial, most authentic ethnic restaurants in town. They are much more apt to offer real food rather than entrées made from salty processed ingredients. Second, order dishes where fresh vegetables are emphasized. Vegetables, as you know, are low in sodium and extremely high in sodium-balancing potassium.

423 ▪ Going Italian? Steer clear of buttery items, heavy tomato sauces, and cheesy pasta dishes. Instead order chicken, veal, fish, or shellfish prepared with garlic and lots of herbs, and add a big, green leafy salad. Flavorful vegetables abound in Italian cooking—choose from broiled mushrooms; sautéed peppers, tomatoes, zucchini, and eggplant; braised spinach or escarole; or steamed artichokes. If you order the artichoke though, skip the butter sauce for dipping and ask for a vinaigrette dressing on the side.

424 ▪ At Greek or Middle Eastern restaurants, order chicken Athenian (Greek lemon-herb chicken), Mediterranean-style fish (broiled with olive oil, garlic, and herbs), broiled lamb chops, meat and vegetable kebabs, or perhaps stuffed grape leaves. Don't forget about salads at Mediterranean restaurants; they're delicious topped with *Tzatziki* sauce (yogurt-cucumber sauce), red wine vinaigrette, or garlic herbed olive oil. If you're sensitive to salt, make it a practice to ask for your salad without olives and feta cheese.

425 ▪ When you visit a French or continental restaurant, look for baked, broiled, poached, or steamed foods. Poached salmon is almost always a winner, but be sure to politely ask for the sauce—whatever it is—on the side. Other recommended entrées include *poulet aux fines herbes* (roast chicken with herbs), fish *en papillote* (fish cooked in its own juices with herbs), sole almondine, steamed mussels, salad *Niçoise* (minus the tuna, if it is canned), or salad *nouvelle* (minus the cheese).

426 ▪ If you like Mexican food, understand that the fillings and sauces in Mexican dishes usually are heavily salted (unless the restaurant makes its food from scratch, in which case you can ask for your entrée to be prepared without salt). To minimize the salt usually used in Mexican restaurants, get into the habit of ordering entrées like burritos, tostadas, or even huevos rancheros without cheese; try a small dab of guacamole, sour cream, or salsa instead for flavor. Fish entrées tend to be some of the lower-sodium picks at Mexican restaurants. Good selections include grilled fish tacos; red snapper or sea bass prepared Veracruz-style (with tomatoes, peppers, and onions); or *camarónes al mojo de ajo* (shrimp sautéed in olive oil with garlic). Although not a truly authentic Mexican food, gazpacho, a refreshing cold vegetable soup, is a healthy choice that can be found in many Mexican restaurants.

427 ▪ **The sodium content of Indian food** varies depending on the restaurant. With tasty spice combinations such as curries, Indian food certainly doesn't need salt, but some restaurants add quite a bit anyway. Call around and see if you can find an Indian restaurant that will cook individual orders without salt if you ask for it. Many are able to honor that request. If not, your best bets to order at Indian restaurants are the simplest entrées—dishes such as chicken or lamb tandoori or korma; chicken or lamb kebabs; or dahl salad (made with bulgur, snow peas, tomato, and olive oil).

428 ▪ **Japanese food tends to be unusually high in salt** and should, for the most part, be avoided. If you do go to a Japanese restaurant, be especially savvy about salt: look on the menu for grilled or steamed fish or ask if hibachi-style entrées can be prepared without the soy sauce and added salt. Also try sushi made from cooked crab and shrimp, or sushi made from vegetables like avocados and cucumbers. A dab or two of wasabi (Japanese horseradish) is all you need to add kick to even the most simply prepared Japanese entrées.

▪ BONUS TIP: *Don't be tempted to try sushi made from raw fish. No matter how meticulously raw fish is prepared, it can be contaminated with parasites. Although raw fish sushi may seem like a novelty worth trying, just a bite of contaminated fish can be dan-*

gerous. Enjoy exotic cuisine without the health risks by sticking with sushi made from vegetables or cooked seafood.

429 ▪ If Chinese food is on the menu, beware. Most Chinese sauces such as hoison, oyster, black bean, and soy sauces are just loaded with salt. Find out what dishes can be made to order and request that no MSG, salt, or any of the sauces listed above be used in your meal. Create tasty combinations by choosing chicken, beef, seafood, or tofu, then combine your choice with vegetables like broccoli, scallions, snow peas, water chestnuts, bean sprouts, bamboo shoots, and bok choy (Chinese cabbage). Ask for your mixture to be stir-fried in peanut, sesame, or canola oil or, even better, order it steamed. To add extra flavor to your meal, request sides of hot mustard, crushed garlic, minced ginger, chopped scallions, and Chinese five-spice powder.

▪ BONUS TIP: *If you suspect that your waiter doesn't understand your request for no MSG in your food, try saying "No may gin" to get your message across.*

ON THE RUN

430 ▪ Fast food is a way of life for many people these days, but understand that most fast food is a disaster in terms of excessive sodium, salt, sugar, and nonessential fat. To get an idea just how high in sodium fast food is, consider this: other than salad, the lowest-sodium choice at the major fast-food chains is a plain hamburger, which by itself has between 500 and 600 milligrams of sodium. (This amount is for the hamburger by itself. If you add a sodium-rich shake and an order of salty fries with ketchup, the sodium content skyrockets, supplying in that one meal much more than some salt-sensitive individuals should have in a single day.) For your best health, try to limit your intake of fast food as much as possible. If you do occasionally eat fast food, ask for a Nutrition Facts brochure at the restaurant and choose the lowest-sodium item possible. Then emphasize low-sodium natural foods the rest of the day to negate the fast-food's high-sodium content.

431 ▪ **Fast-food sandwiches make extremely high-sodium meals.** The bread itself is high in salt, and so are the extras like ketchup, mustard, and mayonnaise. In addition, sodium-rich processed meat products are the rule in fast-food sandwiches. Arby's roast beef, for example, is not real roast beef. It is a processed beef that contains added salt, water, and sodium phosphates. So is the turkey meat in deli sandwiches and the MSG-laced chicken meat in Burger King's BK Broiler Sandwich. When you add up all the unhealthy sodium sources contained in fast-food sandwiches, it's easy to see how one sandwich can single-handedly provide more than half the recommended daily sodium allowance. One of the most effective ways to get the salt out of your diet is to ban fast-food sandwiches from your life.

432 ▪ **Look for prepackaged salads** that are offered at a number of outlets, including some of the bigger fast-food hamburger chains. These often are your best fast-food choices, as long as you avoid the salty dressings that come with them. If you know your schedule necessitates your picking up a salad to go, take along your own dressing (as described in tip 410) to avoid the sodium-rich processed varieties. *One to Three Salt Shakers.*

433 ▪ **Try to find salad bars** where you can choose the items you want so you can have more control over the amount of sodium you consume. When you fill your plate at a salad bar, load up on as many fresh, unprocessed vegetables as you like, but be sure to avoid the high-sodium extras: bacon bits, croutons, pickled foods, mayonnaise-based salads, and premixed salad dressings. This suggestion is helpful to everyone wanting to get the salt out, but particularly for those who are sensitive to MSG. *One to Two Salt Shakers.*

434 ▪ When you have to eat on the run, you can find healthier food at "home-style" fast-food restaurants like Boston Market or Kenny Rogers Roasters, but you still need to be careful about what you order. For example, a roasted chicken pita sandwich may sound healthy, but one offered at Kenny Rogers supplies 1,527 sodium milligrams—three-quarters of the amount most of us need per day. A chicken pot pie also sounds wholesome, but just one pot pie from Boston Market supplies an entire day's worth of sodium (2,380 milligrams)! Fortunately, however, choices are available that are much lower in sodium. The first thing to know is that much of the sodium on rotisserie chicken is on the skin or within the skin itself. If you eat a quarter of either white-meat or dark-meat chicken with the skin removed, and if you also order low-sodium side dishes such as steamed vegetables, baked sweet potato, corn, a side salad, or fruit salad, you can enjoy an entire meal for about 500 milligrams of sodium, a respectable amount that can fit into most low- to moderate-sodium diets. *Three Salt Shakers.*

435 ▪ For an on-the-go snack or mini-meal, try a balanced nutrition bar such as the Balance bar made by BioFoods. Many of my clients enjoy this product because each bar contains a nutrient blend that provides both quick and long-term energy, and it's convenient enough to carry anywhere. It's also healthier than a candy bar and much lower in sodium than fast food or other high-protein snacks such as beef jerky. Look for Balance bars in health food stores or call 1-800-678-7246 to order them directly. *Two Salt Shakers.*

436 ▪ The most comforting fast food for lunch is low-salt soup or leftovers from home. If you invest in a wide-mouthed thermos, you can take your favorite foods to work with you, and lunch will be ready whenever you want it. Homemade foods are much lower in sodium than typical take-out foods and cost a lot less. They're also more satisfying and more nutritious. *One to Two Salt Shakers.*

437 ▪ **Another quick lunch is a Mushroom Broccoli Cheese Muffin, which is a meal in itself;** it serves as a wonderful substitute for a sandwich when you are on the run. If you plan ahead by making a batch of the following muffins ahead of time and then freezing them, you have a ready-to-eat complete meal with each muffin, which you can grab whenever you need. Note that even though the following recipe contains cheese and a small amount of regular butter, one muffin still provides only about one-fifth the sodium found in a regular fast-food burger. (If you want to reduce the sodium content of the muffins further, however, just substitute unsalted butter or olive oil and sodium-reduced cheese in the recipe.) This creative idea and recipe comes from *Smart Muffins* by Jane Kinderlehrer. *Two Salt Shakers.*

▪ MUSHROOM BROCCOLI CHEESE MUFFINS ▪

2 cups lightly steamed chopped broccoli
$^1/_2$ cup grated mozzarella cheese
$^1/_2$ cup chopped onions
1 cup chopped mushrooms
2 tablespoons butter
2 tablespoons whole wheat pastry flour
2 eggs
3 tablespoons wheat germ
4 tablespoons whole wheat flour
$^1/_4$ teaspoon pepper
1 teaspoon crushed oregano
Sesame seeds for garnish

Combine the broccoli and cheese and set aside. Sauté the onions and mushrooms in the butter. Stir in the 2 tablespoons of pastry flour and add $^1/_2$ cup of water. Cook slowly until the sauce thickens.

In a mixing bowl or food processor, blend together the eggs, wheat germ, remaining flour, pepper, and oregano.

Preheat the oven to 400 degrees. Oil 12 regular-size muffin cups and sprinkle the sesame seeds on the bottom of each.

Combine the broccoli-cheese mixture with the other mixture and spoon into the muffin cups. Top each with a sprinkle of sesame seeds (and a pinch of cheese, if desired). Bake for 20 minutes. *Makes 12 muffins.*

438 ▪ **Consider purchasing a small cooler** so you can take low-sodium cold or perishable foods to work with you. (A cooler is especially helpful if you live in a warm climate.) A few ideas of tasty cold lunch items you can carry in a cooler are: Fresh Herbal Tabouli (in tip 202); Salt-Free Sauerkraut (in tip 203); vinaigrette-marinated vegetables; bean salads; salad fixings and salad dressings (like the Reduced Calorie Ranch Dressing in tip 217); vegetable sticks and dip; hard-boiled eggs; cold cooked chicken, turkey, or beef slices; and even leftover Turkey Sausage Pizza (in tip 301). *One to Three Salt Shakers.*

439 ▪ **Carry along low-sodium bottled water with you.** This tip may not seem important, but it is, particularly when you unknowingly consume more sodium than you should while eating on the run. Remember, low-sodium water flushes the system of excess salt and helps to prevent bloating and weight gain from retaining excess water. In addition, bottled water tastes better than tap water, so you'll be apt to drink more of it. It's also better for you. One of the best preventive measures to get the unhealthy salt out of your system (and one of the health-

iest habits in general) is to drink low-sodium bottled (or filtered) water frequently throughout the day. *One Salt Shaker*.

ON THE ROAD

440 ▪ **If you're traveling by car,** bring some low-sodium
meals and snacks with you to avoid grabbing salty foods on the
run. If you have a cooler, pack homemade turkey or roast beef
sandwiches (or any of the other low-sodium sandwich suggestions from the section Sandwich Fixings in chapter 6). If you
don't have a cooler, take along sandwiches made with unsalted
peanut butter. These are simple meals that give you plenty of
staying power.

441 ▪ **When you're out of town** (particularly if you don't
know the area well), it can be a challenge to know where to eat.
When in doubt, go to basic, medium-priced restaurants in the
major hotel chains. You'll usually have much more luck getting
low-salt meals there than you will if you try trendy, indepen-
dent restaurants. Hotel restaurants tend to feature more simple,
basic meals, and they usually do their best at honoring special
requests if they are able to. When you're on the road, remember
that in most cases hotel restaurants are better equipped to prepare food to order. Particularly if the hotel has room service, the
restaurant usually has a full kitchen and staff that can fix food a
number of different ways to cater to its many guests.

▪ BONUS TIP: *Don't forget to take your traveling salt shaker
with you on trips. At times, foods that are prepared without salt may
need a little seasoning, but you certainly don't want to use common
table salt. Carry along healthy salt with you and feel free to add a
dash to bland food without feeling guilty.*

442 ▪ **If you're traveling by plane,** order a special low-salt meal. Most of the major airlines in the United States now have a policy in which no MSG is added to any of their special meals, and that includes the low-sodium or low-salt entrée. Call your airline carrier to be sure of its policy, and place your order directly through the airline or through your travel agent every time you reserve your ticket. If you're sensitive to salt or MSG, taking the time to order a special meal just may prevent you from developing uncomfortable bloating, an allergic headache, or other troublesome symptoms while traveling. To prevent any mishaps, double-check on your special meal a day before your departure.

▪ BONUS TIP: *Though a fresh fruit plate is certain to be low in sodium, nutritious, and refreshing, an entire meal based on fruit can cause a blood sugar high followed by a blood sugar low, leaving you feeling lethargic an hour or two after eating. To give you the extended energy you need for long trips, order a well-balanced special meal that contains protein. You often will receive fresh fruit for dessert. If you're extremely sensitive to salt or MSG, your safest choice may be a fruit plate, but eat only a small amount of fruit and make most of your meal high-protein snacks that you bring yourself. (See tip 443 for details.) Give the rest of the fruit on your plate to a traveling companion, or stuff some of the harder fruits (such as apples) in your carrying bag for later.*

443 ▪ **Take high-quality mini-meals with you on the plane** to sustain you if the airline gives you a meal you would rather not eat. High-protein snacks that are great for traveling are 3-ounce pop-top cans of low-sodium tuna, sandwiches made from unsalted nut butter, and the Mushroom Broccoli Cheese Muffins in tip 437.

444 ▪ **Also bring low-sodium snacks with you** to replace the salty pretzels and roasted nuts commonly served on airplane flights. Take unsalted whole grain pretzels, or an assortment of homemade, oven-toasted nuts. These choices won't leave you feeling deprived when you pass up the overly salted snacks handed to you on planes. You'll also cut the salt by hundreds of milligrams. Other good snacks for trips are low-sodium, low-sugar muffins (like the Wheat-Free Banana Muffins in tip 142) and trail mixes (made with a variety of nuts and unsulphured fruits). *One to Two Salt Shakers.*

445 ▪ **As always, the best drink to order on airplane flights** is low-sodium bottled water. Proper hydration with low-sodium water is always important for getting the salt out, but it is especially important when flying. I find that having low-sodium, quality water is so crucial to my feeling my best when I'm traveling that I make it a point to take a bottle with me in my carry-on. *One Salt Shaker.*

446 ▪ **If you're planning a cruise,** call your cruise line ahead of time to request a special diet menu low in salt. To both keep the salt out and the weight off, your best choices on board are broiled, baked, or poached meats, poultry, or fish accompanied by steamed vegetables and a green salad.

▪ BONUS TIP: *Whether you take the time to order a special menu or not, be careful not to let eating become a full-time occupation while you're on board. Relax and enjoy yourself during the cruise, but eat simply and exercise a lot to prevent gaining weight. Taking a cruise should be a relaxing, health-enhancing experience, not an excuse to overindulge in salty foods and come back feeling worse than you did before you left.*

CHAPTER 10

Get the Salt Out
of Your Life

Making a commitment to keep unhealthy sodium out of your diet is a challenge. Although your sodium needs may change during different stages of life, your resolve to avoid unhealthy sodium should remain constant. Keeping that resolve isn't always easy, of course. Physically, your body may crave salt because it's deficient in nutrients. Emotionally, you may be tempted by salty snacks when you're stressed. Socially, everyone from your kids to your best friends may try to coax you into eating salty foods because "everyone else does." Also, because the issue of dietary salt doesn't yet have the widespread media attention that fat and sugar do, you may sometimes feel a bit different from the rest of the public because you have more awareness than most people do of the hazards of refined salt. Learning to cope with these various pressures is difficult, but it is something you need to learn. So important are these personal concerns that if you know how to avoid salt in the foods you eat but never address the personal pressures you face, the chances are not good that your dietary change will last.

That's because your beliefs, thoughts, and feelings influence your actions. The mind-body connection is so strong that some researchers say altering attitude does, in fact, alter behavior. My professional experience bears this out. Thinking back about the thousands of clients I have seen, I can honestly tell you that those who have made the most positive and lasting dietary changes were the ones whose attitudes underwent health-enhancing transformations as well.

This final chapter discusses how to cope with all the impediments you may face in your journey to get the salt out. It includes ways to overcome problems with others as well as troubles with yourself. It also covers other important health topics like stress, exercise, and weight loss. Although these subjects seem unrelated, you will see that they all play a part in your keeping the salt out and staying healthy in general.

GETTING STARTED

447 ▪ **Start by eliminating the sodium sources that you are the least apt to miss.** This means processed and packaged foods that contain hidden sodium additives as well as those that contain hidden salt in combination with hidden sugar.

448 ▪ **Gradually wean yourself away from typically salty foods** by switching to lower-sodium, healthier, sea-salted products found in health food stores.

449 ▪ **Stay in close contact with your doctor,** especially if you are currently taking medication. If you cut the salt in your diet in a noticeable way, your blood pressure could change dramatically, and some ailments, such as migraines or bloating from water retention, may be alleviated. Your medication, therefore, may need to be reduced or even eliminated.

450 ▪ **Cut out sodium-rich medicines** such as the

antacids Alka-Seltzer and Bromo-Seltzer. With 995 sodium milligrams per two-tablet dose of Alka-Seltzer and 761 sodium milligrams in one tablet of Bromo-Seltzer, these ill-advised medicines contribute more sodium to your diet than many fast foods.

451 ▪ **Get rid of other unnecessary sodium sources in your life.** Common commercial toothpaste, for example, contains sodium saccharin, a substance that has been shown to cause cancer in rats. Avoid this unhealthy source of sodium by switching to a toothpaste that has no saccharin, such as Tom's of Maine.

452 ▪ **Another surprising source of sodium** is the glue on the back of postage stamps. If you're stamping a lot of letters, it makes sense to use a sponge.

453 ▪ **If simply out of habit you shake more salt on your food than you should,** tape over some of the holes on your salt shaker to cut down on the sodium you consume and to gradually reeducate your taste buds to enjoy less salt.

454 ▪ **Keep a food diary.** Many of my clients think their diets are healthy until I ask them to keep food diaries. Then they start to see the truth of what they're really eating. I encourage you to try this valuable experience: jot down everything you eat and drink for a week or two and honestly appraise how low your salt intake actually is.

455 ▪ **Look for patterns in your food record,** particularly in regard to when you crave and indulge in salt. Some of the patterns I have seen among my clients are that they tend to want to binge on salty junk food when they're overworked or overstressed, and many eat more salt than they should on weekends. Knowing your body's tendencies is tremendously useful: if you pinpoint the kinds of personal situations in which you have trouble avoiding salt, you will be much better prepared to handle them in the future.

456 ▪ **If you like to keep numerical count of the sodium milligrams you ingest,** buy yourself a clear, easy-to-follow sodium counter and familiarize yourself with it. A number of books of this sort are available. One I often use for reference is *The Sodium Counter* by Annette B. Natow, Ph.D., R.D., and Jo-Ann Heslin, M.A., R.D.

▪ BONUS TIP: *Sodium counters can help you understand why you should eat naturally because they statistically show you how much higher in sodium processed and fast foods are than natural foods. The biggest drawback of sodium counters, however, is that they usually don't list the sodium content of the healthier food options carried in natural food stores. You can use them to learn about the sodium content of commercial foods (the ones you want to avoid), but understand that they don't represent many of the lower-sodium foods available to you.*

457 ▪ **Use cookbooks that support your conviction to get the salt out.** When you do something new, it always helps to have references that show you how to do it. Although you can adapt your old recipes to lower their salt content, you may find it easier to keep to your new way of eating if you start anew with low-salt cookbooks in combination with the recipes in this book.

458 ▪ **Learn all you can about herbs and spices.** Take a cooking class that emphasizes using herbs or treat yourself to books or magazines that give you insights on how to use herbs. Think about your new way of cooking not so much as a way to get the salt out but as an opportunity to learn an important new skill: how to put more flavorful seasonings in!

▪ ▪ ▪

DEALING WITH STRESS

459 ▪ **The body's response to stress is intimately connected to the body's use of salt.** As I explained in the Preface, it is possible to eat a diet extremely low in sodium diet and yet have high levels of sodium in the body. This is because stress alone can cause the body to retain sodium. To really get the salt out of your life and prevent it from harming your body, you must do more than limit salt in your diet: you also must conquer the stress you feel in your life. If you overcome or reduce stress, you give your adrenal glands a break so they can better balance the body's sodium levels. The following are some tips to help you do this:

460 ▪ **Continually remind yourself that worrying won't change what's happening in your life,** but it will take its toll on your health. (It may be as harmful to you as consuming excess sodium.) The best way to alter the physical effects of worrying is to change your attitude: do your best in a given situation, but then put the subject out of your mind and trust that things will work out in the end.

461 ▪ **Take some time every day for R and R** (rest and relaxation). Reflection is also helpful, too. You need to nourish the spirit as much as you do the body.

462 ▪ **If you have high blood pressure or have trouble letting go of tension,** it's particularly important to learn a relaxation technique. Popular forms of relaxation include: yoga, deep-breathing exercises, biofeedback, progressive relaxation technique, and meditation.

463 ▪ **Treat yourself to a massage.** Whether given by a professional or your lover, a massage can do wonders for releasing stored tensions.

464 ▪ **Learn to share your feelings,** both negative and positive, with your family, friends, and health-care providers. Releasing pent-up anger and frustrations makes you feel better emotionally, and it sometimes improves physical conditions like high blood pressure as well.

465 ▪ **Try homeopathic and Bach Flower Remedies,** which can be found in health food stores. During times of stress, these safe, gentle, natural aids can offer relief, and some of my clients swear by them. One particular product worth noting is Rescue Remedy, which is made from a combination of distilled flower essences. Taken under the tongue or in water, Rescue Remedy helps during any type of trauma, be it emotional, mental, or physical.

466 ▪ **Use fragrances to relax you.** Several clients have told me that the smells of lavender and chamomile help calm them.

467 ▪ **Soak in a sudsy, warm bath** and let your troubles wash away.

468 ▪ **Or commune with nature.** It's healing for many people.

469 ▪ **It doesn't matter how you relax, only that you do.** Determine which relaxation techniques work the best for you and use them often. Just as your diet should be personalized, so too should your stress-reduction program.

470 ▪ **Avoid substances that infringe on the adrenal glands' ability to cope with stress.** The top three dietary substances that do this are caffeine, alcohol, and sugar.

471 ▪ **Nourish your adrenal glands with supplements.** Many people (including myself) find they cope with stress far more effectively when they provide the hard-working adrenal glands with extra support. One product I have found particularly helpful in this regard is an adrenal glandular complex called the Uni Key Adrenal Formula. With vitamins, minerals, and adrenal glandular tissue, it contains all the elements the body needs to deal with stress more effectively.

NUTRIENT NECESSITIES

472 ▪ If you get salt cravings occasionally, they probably are due to stress. To stave off stress-induced cravings, try taking 500-milligram tablets of pantothenic acid several times daily. Pantothenic acid, the official name for vitamin B-5, is food for the adrenal glands, and during times of stress, the adrenals' need for pantothenic acid skyrockets. In his book *No More Cravings* (Warner Books, 1987), Douglas Hunt, M.D., reports that pantothenic acid supplementation gives immediate relief to his patients who suffer from stress-related salt cravings.

473 ▪ Other nutrients that fight stress and can be helpful are the B-complex vitamins (known as the "antistress" vitamins), vitamin C, zinc, and manganese. For nutritional fortification against stress, choose an adrenal-supportive supplement that contains a combination of these beneficial nutrients.

474 ▪ If you have trouble tasting salt, it may be because your diet is lacking in zinc. Zinc deficiency is much more common than once thought, appearing in 68 percent of the American population and in a much higher percentage of the senior citizen population. Zinc is a mineral that is essential for developing a keen sense of taste and smell, and when it is lacking, many individuals need to add more and more salt, to be able to taste their food. I believe this deficiency is a primary reason for our country's overconsumption of salt, so I recommend at least 30 milligrams supplemental zinc daily.

475 ▪ **If you take calcium or other bone-building supplements** because you want to prevent osteoporosis, remember that one of the most effective things you can do for your bones is to reduce your salt intake. Several studies have shown that excessive salt causes a breakdown of bone and an increased loss of calcium in the urine. These two factors greatly increase the risk of developing osteoporosis.

▪ BONUS TIP: *Besides cutting down your salt intake, you can also improve your calcium status by avoiding the following: soft drinks; caffeine; smoking cigarettes; eating an excessively high-protein diet; and eating a diet high in grains and foods that contain oxalates (cocoa, asparagus, sorrel, rhubarb, spinach, and dandelion greens). As I explained in my book* Super Nutrition for Women *(Bantam Books, 1991), all of these factors adversely affect calcium metabolism and absorption and increase the chances of developing a calcium deficiency.*

476 ▪ **Watch out for supplements that contain salt.** Glucosamine sulfate, for example, is a popular product taken by many arthritis sufferers and athletes with injuries, but many brands of this supplement contain a hidden dose of sodium chloride in addition to the glucosamine. (The hidden sodium is disguised as the ingredient NaCl sulfate on the label.) If you use glucosamine sulfate, look for brands that are sodium-free and that list 2 KCl instead of 2 NaCl in the ingredients. When you look for a multiple vitamin, select one that is salt-free.

▪ BONUS TIP: *The only kinds of supplements in which sodium is necessary are electrolyte replacement supplements, which are often needed by those who exercise strenuously. See tip 479 for more information.*

▪ ▪ ▪

THE ACTIVE INGREDIENT

477 ▪ Exercise gets the salt out. Any activity in which you work up a sweat causes you to lose sodium through perspiration. If you accidentally overindulge in salt, you can use exercise as a way to normalize your sodium levels.

478 ▪ Exercise increases your need for sodium, but don't use it as an excuse to eat junk food high in refined salt and sodium additives. Sensibly replenish the extra sodium you need for exercise by emphasizing the higher-sodium vegetables listed in tip 67 or the seaweeds listed in tip 61, and by adding a few extra shakes of unrefined sea salt or Real Salt to your food.

479 ▪ Better yet, increase your intake of all electrolytes (minerals that are necessary for proper muscle functioning and fluid balance). Because exercise increases your need for other minerals like calcium, magnesium, and potassium, adding extra salt alone to your diet may not be enough to replace what is lost during heavy exercise. (As you know, imprudent use of salt also can create mineral imbalance in the body.) If you are involved in strenuous athletics, if you exercise frequently, or if you do heavy work outside in a hot climate, I recommend electrolyte replacement supplements. They supply other necessary minerals, such as potassium, which help balance the extra sodium athletes require.

480 ▪ Why exercise regularly? One of the most important reasons is because physical activity is very effective for reducing stress: it relieves irritability, anxiety, and depression, and helps create a feeling of emotional well-being. As you will recall from Dealing with Stress, the previous section, reducing stress normalizes sodium levels.

481 ▪ Exercise's other benefits also might make you a

convert. It reduces the risk of death in men from all causes by 70 percent and lessens the risk of heart attack by 39 percent. It also helps prevent and alleviate high blood pressure (a fact that I'm sure is appreciated by everyone who wants to get the salt out). Other advantages of physical activity include:

increased circulation	improved appetite
increased oxygenation	better digestion
cardiovascular toning	improved eliminations
regulation of the glandular system	enhanced immunity
lowered cholesterol	increased self-esteem
increased confidence	enhanced metabolic rate
stronger bones and muscles	control of blood sugar levels
regulation of insulin production	increased flexibility

(List adapted from my book *Super Nutrition for Men*)

Make no mistake about it: regular exercise helps you not only get the salt out but also is one of the best overall ways to promote your health that you can do!

■ BONUS TIP: *Take mini-exercise breaks at work. Stretch, touch your toes, do knee bends, and even calisthenics for five or ten minutes instead of taking a coffee break. Even this small bit of activity promotes a mental lift and a sense of calmness and "centeredness."*

SLIM FOR KEEPS

482 ■ **An added benefit of salt restriction is weight loss.** Salt is so known for causing water retention and weight gain that many health spas have a policy in which no salt is used in food preparation. The miraculous weight loss experienced by many spa guests after a few days is mainly because their salt intake has been restricted. If you avoid salt at home, you can accomplish the same results as the spas do (without the hefty spa bill).

483 ▪ **If you are overweight,** it's especially important for you to get the salt out. Reducing salt can decrease an average person's weight by as much as two to three pounds in one day, but it can drop a severely obese individual's weight as much as ten pounds in a single day.

484 ▪ **If you're sensitive to salt or suffer from edema,** use the following clues and symptoms as signals to tell you that you've eaten too much salt:

> pants that fit well yesterday but don't fit today
> sore, swollen ankles
> a puffy face
> shoes that you wear every day suddenly becoming too
>   tight
> fingers that are so swollen you are unable to take off your
>   rings

If you experience any of these, know that they are telltale signs that your body wants you to get the salt out.

485 ▪ **Say "no thanks" to so-called "diet shakes."** They stress the body's metabolism more than help it, and they couldn't possibly help you lose fat because they're sources of undesirable sodium and sugar. (They may, however, cause you to lose muscle mass, which is exactly what you *don't* want.) With some varieties containing caffeine and other varieties containing as much as 460 milligrams of sodium and 33 grams of sugar, these shakes act as antinutrients and are just plain dangerous.

486 ▪ **Despite what you might have heard, lean meat is not high in sodium nor is it fattening.** Although animal protein is higher in sodium than fruits and vegetables, it still is low in sodium. Contrary to popular belief, eating animal protein in moderation also encourages weight loss. First, protein-rich meat promotes proper fluid balance. If protein is lacking in the diet, water retention and water weight gain develop. More importantly, protein-rich meat stimulates fat loss. It causes the body to produce glucagon, and glucagon is a hormone that allows the body to efficiently burn off its stored fat for energy. To encourage efficient weight loss, include at least two servings of animal protein each day, and always balance the protein with lots of salad or low-starch vegetables.

▪ BONUS TIP: *Don't eat large servings of luncheon meats as a way to increase your protein intake. Processed meat products like these have as much as ten to fifteen times the sodium as fresh meats. Eating these meats encourages water weight gain instead of weight loss.*

THE REST OF THE WORLD

487 ▪ Enlist the assistance of others to help you get the salt out. Try going on the buddy system with a friend or family member who also is reducing their salt intake. The support and camaraderie of having someone else in your shoes makes eliminating salt easier, much more fun, and usually more successful.

488 ▪ **Hire a qualified nutritionist,** especially if you have severe salt cravings.

489 ▪ **Play a game with your children** by challenging them to help you find acceptable low-sodium foods in the grocery store. They usually enjoy helping you and think the game is fun. They also learn a lot about food (and how much salt and sodium there is in food) in the process.

490 ▪ Start feeding your children unsalted foods when they're babies. You'll give them a healthier start and prevent them from developing a potentially dangerous desire for excessive salt, which would cause problems later on in life. Don't think keeping salt away from children isn't helpful for their health: studies with animals suggest that babies are less capable of excreting excess salt than adults. In addition, high-sodium intakes early in life may predispose babies to developing hypertension as adults.

▪ BONUS TIP: *As further proof that low-sodium nutrition is best for babies, consider that human milk, the ideal food for infants, naturally contains a low amount of sodium, regardless of how much salt the mother eats. By comparison, cow's milk, which is ideal for calves, contains 600 percent more salt.*

491 ▪ The best way to guarantee that a child won't become addicted to salt is for that child to have a parent who isn't. Get the salt out of your diet and let your child learn by example.

492 ▪ Don't give your child salty snacks as rewards, and ask the same of day care providers, teachers, and relatives. Remember, a liking for excessive salt is a learned behavior, so it's important not only to encourage them in their efforts but also to *discourage* your children from indulging in salt.

493 ▪ Be creative when packing your children's school lunches by providing low-sodium, nutritious foods that their friends would want, too. One snack food that certainly fits that description is unsalted blue or red tortilla chips. If you pack fun, novel, tasty foods like these, you certainly will encourage your children to eat low-salt foods, and you may unknowingly influence your children's friends as well!

494 ▪ **Add spice to life by planning fun times with interesting people.** If you find yourself wanting the taste excitement of salt, consider whether you don't really want emotional or mental stimulation instead.

HEALTHY ATTITUDES, HEALTHY LIFE

495 ▪ **Don't get discouraged. Persevere,** even when it seems like everyone around you is eating too much salt. You have to understand that you now know a secret that many others have yet to learn: maintaining discipline over your intake of salt and unhealthy sodium is an important key to long-lasting health. Continue to remind yourself of this.

496 ▪ **Reinforce your commitment to eat healthfully** as much as you need to in order to ensure success. One technique that works well is to post on your refrigerator positive affirmations as well as a list of the many reasons you want to avoid salt. Then every time you begin to open the refrigerator door, you receive helpful reminders about why you want to keep the salt out.

497 ▪ **Envision yourself easily being in control of the salt you consume** and having a healthy attitude about food in general. Positive mental images often translate into positive results.

498 ▪ **Concentrate on improving yourself,** even when others close to you are not interested in doing the same. If others see how helpful reducing salt is for you, they might follow your lead. Even if they don't, you need to do what's right for you. Your primary responsibility in life is to be the best person (physically, mentally, and spiritually) that you can be.

499 ▪ Do things you haven't done before. Foods loaded with salt no longer seem so necessary when you give yourself the "charge" of stimulating, new activities.

500 ▪ Value yourself enough to nourish yourself with life-giving whole foods (instead of eating life-draining processed foods, as so many Americans do). Certain cultures, such as some Native American tribes and the Chinese, believe that both plant-based and animal-based whole foods have a life force that strengthens our own life force when we use those foods for nourishment. As you've learned, natural foods like these also help support good health because they're low in sodium but otherwise dense with nutrients.

501 ▪ Treat yourself to experiences you can savor many years from now. In the long run, the things you remember are not the salty foods you've eaten but the warm, meaningful experiences you've shared with people you love.

AFTERWORD

These days, advice about sodium can be as misguided as all the conflicting advice about fat.

Although Americans know the hazards of too much fat in the diet all too well, many still eat too many processed foods with the wrong kinds of fat and too few natural foods with the right kinds of fat. This same situation, unfortunately, is also happening with sodium.

Get the Salt Out was written to set the record straight: the truth is that we all need sodium, but too much of the wrong kinds can cause disease. The sodium found in natural foods is a good source of sodium that helps support good health. However, refined table salt, which is found in virtually every processed food and salt shaker across the land, is not.

In this day and age, when fat is wrongly blamed for all our health problems, it's often easy to forget that table salt truly is bad for us. There is no doubt, however, that table salt is a real villain that contributes to serious disease.

Now that you know this and you know the secrets of how to get salt out of your diet, it's your responsibility to use this information to your advantage and become a food consumer who is seasoned as well as savvy about salt.

APPENDIX

The following sample menus for a week represent one way to incorporate this book's low-salt tips into everyday eating. It's meant to provide you with meal and snack ideas, not something that should be followed to the letter.

The sum of the amount of sodium in the food on each day's menu totals less than 1,500 milligrams of sodium—an amount that is appropriate for most people on a low-sodium diet. If you want a more moderate sodium intake or if you have higher sodium needs because of specific physical conditions, you should add extra salt at the table to meet your requirements.

Even if you're on a low-sodium diet, you still can enjoy foods you may have thought were forbidden. This menu shows you that foods such as pizza, pretzels, and even sauerkraut can all be included, as long as you are careful about using any salt when you prepare or select them.

This menu illustrates how to include many tasty foods you'll relish, but it may not be your ideal eating program. The secret of developing a low-salt diet you can stick to is to personalize what you have learned about salt and create an eating plan that works for you.

▪ MONDAY ▪

Breakfast—Cream of rye cereal topped with crushed caraway seeds and homemade yogurt cheese (see tip 140)
$1/3$ cantaloupe

Lunch—Lean homemade roast beef sandwich on salt-free rye bread with sliced onions, red leaf lettuce, and a dab of Instant Horse-radish Sauce (see tip 293)
$1/2$ cup Salt-Free Sauerkraut (see tip 203)
2 unsalted whole-grain pretzel twists dabbed with unsalted mustard

Dinner—Sole almondine (3 ounces baked sole topped with a table-spoon of toasted slivered almonds and a dash of almond oil)
Steamed green beans
Baked Apples with Walnuts, Raisins, Cinnamon, and Nutmeg (see tip 378)

▪ TUESDAY ▪

Breakfast—1 hard-boiled egg sprinkled with salt-free herbal blend and freshly ground black pepper
$1/2$ cup oatmeal topped with 1 tablespoon toasted pecans, 1 tea-spoon currants, and 1 teaspoon pure maple syrup

Lunch—1 cup Spring Minestrone (see tip 187)
$1/2$ cup Fresh Herbal Tabouli (see tip 202)

Snack   A few low-sodium, whole grain, bible bread (sprouted) wedges dipped in Winter Bean Pâté (see tip 357)

Dinner—2 broiled lamb chops with rosemary or oregano leaves and garlic, sprinkled liberally with fresh lemon juice
1 cup Greek-Style Spinach and Brown Rice (see tip 255)

▪ WEDNESDAY ▪

Breakfast—Shredded wheat or other low-sodium, sugar-free, ready-to-eat cereal topped with ¹/₂ sliced banana, 1 tablespoon toasted hazelnuts, and ¹/₂ cup nonfat milk

Lunch—Grilled Mexican Turkey Burger (see tip 232) with lime wedge
Grilled zucchini slices brushed with olive oil and sprinkled with garlic powder
1 cup unsalted baked corn tortilla chips dipped into Simple South-of-the-Border Salsa (see tip 339)

Dinner—Mixed green salad with shredded carrot and green pepper slices topped with Sesame-Lemon Dressing (see tip 210)
Spicy Thai Shrimp Soup with Fresh Cilantro (see tip 185)

▪ THURSDAY ▪

Breakfast—2 slices low-sodium, whole grain sourdough toast spread lightly with unsalted peanut butter
Sliced pear

Lunch—Vegetarian Chili (see tip 260)
15 small grapes

Snack   1 Mushroom Broccoli Cheese Muffin (see tip 437)

Dinner—Spiced Beef with Wine, Ginger, and Garlic (see tip 229)
Sesame Broccoli and Carrots (see tip 275)

▪ FRIDAY ▪

Breakfast—2 Low-Sodium Turkey Sausage patties (see tip 157)
1 Wheat-Free Banana Muffin (see tip 142)

Lunch—T.L.T. Sandwich (see tip 316)
1 no-salt-added pickle

Dinner—Tandoori Chicken (see tip 236)
  $^1/_2$ cup brown basmati rice made in low-sodium or homemade chicken broth with a pinch of saffron
  $^1/_2$ cup unsweetened pineapple chunks

▪ SATURDAY ▪

Brunch—$^1/_2$ grapefruit
  2 eggs (or 1 egg and 2 egg whites) scrambled together with chopped tomato, peppers, onion, and marjoram
  $^1/_2$ cup baked home fries made with 1 tablespoon olive oil and sprinkled with onion powder and a dash of cayenne

Snack—$^1/_4$ Turkey Sausage Pizza (see tip 301) *or* a serving of Nachos (see tip 304)
  Romaine lettuce salad with chopped radish and jicama topped with Herb Dressing (see tip 208)

Snack—3 celery sticks spread with unsalted cashew butter

Dinner—Poached salmon fillet topped with a tablespoon of Greek Tzatziki Sauce (see tip 294)
  Steamed artichoke with low-sodium herbal vinaigrette
  $^1/_2$ cup steamed asparagus spears sprinkled with tarragon vinegar or other herbed vinegar

▪ **SUNDAY** ▪

Breakfast—Annette's Oatmeal Waffles (see tip 146) topped with
$1/4$ cup unsweetened applesauce *or* 1 sliced fresh peach

Lunch—Homemade salad Niçoise with $3^1/2$ ounces low-sodium
canned tuna; $1/2$ cup steamed and cooled diced potatoes; $1/2$ cup
steamed and cooled French-cut green beans; $1/4$ cucumber,
peeled, seeded, and diced; $1/4$ chopped tomato; and chopped
fresh parsley topped with a low-sodium herbal vinaigrette

Dinner—Roast Cornish hen meat rubbed with sage
Baked sweet potato with 1 teaspoon unsalted butter and a
sprinkling of cinnamon
Steamed cauliflower or brussels sprouts sprinkled with salt-free
dill seasoning

RESOURCES

BIOFORCE OF AMERICA, LTD.
P.O. Box 507
Kinderhook, NY 12106
(800) 445-8802

This company distributes the herbal salts Herbamare and Trocomare, mentioned in tip 59. Unlike other herbal salts, these products are made from unrefined sea salt that is cured with dehydrated vegetables and herbs. They are available in several different sizes, including a handy 3.2-ounce shaker that is easy to carry with you to restaurants.

FRENCH MEADOW BAKERY
2610 Lyndale Avenue South
Minneapolis, MN 55408
(612) 870-4740

French Meadow Bakery is the only company I know of that makes naturally low-sodium sourdough bread with unrefined sea salt. It also makes salt-free rye bread. All of these delicious, healthful products are available through mail order if you are unable to find them in health food stores.

THE GRAIN AND SALT SOCIETY
P.O. Box DD
Magalia, CA 95954
(916) 872-5800

This organization sells unrefined Celtic sea salt, which is available through mail order only. It also distributes valuable information about the health benefits of unrefined sea salt.

LANG NATURALS
850 Aquidneck Avenue
Newport, RI 02842
(800) Sauce-4-U
(800) 728-2348

Lang Naturals is the manufacturer of the nine different award-winning Mr. Spice sauces, which are free of salt, MSG, and sodium. If you're on a low-sodium diet, or if you're just looking for tasty low-sodium condiments, these sauces are worth seeking out. Call the company to find a location in your area that sells them or to order them directly.

REDMOND MINERALS
P.O. Box 219
Redmond, UT 84652
(800) 367-7258

The maker of Real Salt, this company also sells an ultra-small convenient salt shaker that is perfect for all your dining-out and traveling needs. If you can't find Real Salt, or if you would like to try the traveling Real Salt shaker that I so highly recommend (particularly if you eat out often), call the company directly and ask about its special introductory offer.

If you're on a low-sodium diet, or if you're just looking for tasty low-sodium condiments, these sauces are worth seeking out. Call the company to find a location in your area that sells them or to order them directly.

THE SPICE HUNTER
254 Granada Drive
San Luis Obispo, CA 93401
(800) 444-3061

The Spice Hunter manufactures a complete line of bottled salt-free seasonings and dried herbs as well as salt-free seasoning packets for dips, salad dressings, Indian food, and dishes such as fajitas, tacos, and meatloaf. Call to locate a health food store or specialty supermarket near you that carries these helpful seasonings.

UNI KEY HEALTH SYSTEMS
P.O. Box 7168
Bozeman, MT 59771
(800) 888-4353

Uni Key is a source for many innovative products. It also distributes quality supplements like the Uni Key Adrenal Formula as well as all of my books. Ask for a brochure about all the latest products.

GMX INTERNATIONAL
(909) 627-5700

GMX International manufactures and distributes magnetic water conditioning systems, a salt-free solution to treating hard water for residential and commercial applications. GMX systems have been proven effective by both university testing and thousands of satisfied customers.

BIBLIOGRAPHY

Arizona Heart Institute Foundation. *Arizona Heart Institute Foundation Cookbook: A Renaissance in Good Eating.* Phoenix, AZ: AHIF, 1993.

Bagg, Elma W. *Cooking without a Grain of Salt.* New York: Bantam Books, 1972.

Blaylock, Russell L., M.D. *Excitotoxins: The Taste That Kills.* Santa Fe, NM: Health Press, 1994.

Bragg, Paul C., and Patricia Bragg. *Gourmet Health Recipes.* Santa Barbara, CA: Health Science, 1992.

Brunswick, J. Peter, Dorothy Love, and Asa Weinberg, M.D. *How to Live 365 Days a Year the Salt-Free Way.* New York: Bantam Books, 1977.

Cleveland, Lucia McMillan. *The Spice Hunter Recipe Collection.* San Louis Obispo: The Spice Hunter, 1989.

Crook, William G., M.D., and Marjorie Hurt Jones, R.N. *The Yeast Connection Cookbook.* Jackson, TN: Professional Books, 1989.

de Langre, Jacques, Ph.D. *Sea Salt's Hidden Powers.* Magalia, CA: Happiness Press, 1992.

Dranov, Paula. "The Surprising Salt Shake-Up." *Good Housekeeping.* August 1995, 60, 62.

Eaton, S. Boyd, M.D., Marjorie Shostak, and Melvin Konner, Ph.D. *The Paleolithic Prescription.* New York: Harper & Row, 1988.

Eck, Dr. Paul C., and Dr. Larry Wilson. *Nutritional Aspects of Stress.* A reference sheet from The Eck Institute of Applied Nutrition and Bioenergetics, 1988.

Fowler, George, and Jeff Lehr. *Feed Your Soul.* New York: Fireside Books, 1993.

Gates, Donna. *The Body Ecology Diet.* Atlanta, GA: B.E.D. Publications, 1993.

Gilbertie, Sal. *Kitchen Herbs.* New York: Bantam Books, 1988.

Gittleman, Ann Louise, M.S. *Beyond Pritikin.* New York: Bantam Books, 1988.

———. *Get the Sugar Out.* New York: Crown Publishers, 1996.

———. *Super Nutrition for Men.* New York: M. Evans and Company, 1996.

———. *Super Nutrition for Menopause.* New York: Pocket Books, 1993.

———. *Super Nutrition for Women.* New York: Bantam Books, 1991.

———. *Your Body Knows Best.* New York: Pocket Books, 1996.

Hunt, Douglas, M.D. *No More Cravings.* New York: Warner Books, 1987.

Hurley, Judith Benn. *The Good Herb.* New York: William Morrow and Company, 1995.

Jones, Jeanne. *Food Lover's Diet.* New York: Charles Scribner's Sons, 1982.

———. *Secrets of Salt-Free Cooking.* San Francisco, CA: 101 Productions, 1981.

Jordan, Peg, R.N. *How the New Food Labels Can Save Your Life.* Studio City, CA: Michael Weise Productions, 1994.

Kinderlehrer, Jane. *Smart Chicken.* New York: Newmarket Press, 1991.

———. *Smart Muffins.* New York: Newmarket Press, 1987.

Lake, Rhody. "Magnetized Water Is No Mystery." *Alive.* No. 148, 12.

Lakhani, the Kitchen of Mrs. *Indian Recipes for a Healthy Heart.* Los Angeles, CA: Fahil Publishing Company, 1991.

Liebman, Bonnie F., Dr. Michael Jacobsen, and Greg Moyer. *Salt: The Brand Name Guide to Sodium Content.* New York: Warner Books, 1983.

Mindell, Earl, Ph.D. *Safe Eating.* New York: Warner Books, 1987.

"Miso: High in Protein and Flavor." *Natural Health Shopper.* December 1995, 8.

Moore, Richard D. *The High Blood Pressure Solution: Natural Protection and Cure with the K Factor.* Rochester, VT: Healing Arts Press, 1993.

Murray, Michael T., N.D. *Natural Alternatives to Over-the-Counter and Prescription Drugs.* New York: William Morrow and Company, 1994.

Murray, Michael T., N.D., and the Nutrition Department of Trillium Health Products. *The Healing Power of Foods Cookbook.* Rocklin, CA: Prima Publishing, 1993.

Natow, Annette B., Ph.D., R.D., and Jo-Ann Heslin, M.A., R.D. *The Sodium Counter.* New York: Pocket Books, 1993.

Nostrand, Carol A. *Junk Food to Real Food.* New Canaan, CT: Keats Publishing, 1994.

Pannell, Maggie. *High Blood Pressure Special Diet Cookbook.* Wellingborough, Northamptonshire, England: Thorsons Publishing Group, 1991.

Pitchford, Paul. *Healing with Whole Foods.* Berkeley, CA: North Atlantic Books, 1993.

Rector-Page, Linda. *Cooking for Healthy Healing.* Sonora, CA: Healthy Healing Publications, 1991.

Remington, Dennis W., M.D., and Barbara W. Higa, R.D. *Back to Health.* Provo, UT: Vitality House International, Inc., 1986.

Roth, Harriet. *Deliciously Low.* New York: New American Library, 1983.

———. *Deliciously Simple.* New York: Plume Books, 1988.

Schauss, Alexander, Barbara Friedlander Meyer, and Arnold Meyer. *Eating for A's.* New York: Pocket Books, 1991.

Schwartz, George R. *In Bad Taste: The MSG Syndrome.* New York: Signet Books, 1990.

Starke, Rodman D., and Mary Winston, Ed.D., R.D., eds. *The American Heart Association Low-Salt Cookbook*. New York: Random House, 1990.

Vaughan, Dr. William J. *Low Salt Secrets for Your Diet*. New York: Warner Books, 1981.

Weil, Andrew, M.D. *Natural Health, Natural Medicine*. Boston: Houghton Mifflin Company, 1990.

Weiner, Michael A., Ph.D. *Healing Children Naturally*. San Rafael, CA: Quantum Books, 1982.

Whittlesey, Marietta. *Killer Salt*. New York: Avon Books, 1977.

PERMISSIONS

"Almond Macaroon Adaptation Recipe." Reprinted by permission of Melissa Diane Smith.

"Annette's Oatmeal Waffles" from *Back to Health*, by Dennis Remington and Barbara W. Higa, R.D. Copyright © 1986 by Dennis Remington and Barbara W. Higa, R.D. Reprinted by permission of Vitality House International, Inc.

"Baked Apples with Raisins, Cinnamon, and Nutmeg" from *Beyond Pritikin*, by Ann Louise Gittleman, M.S. Copyright © 1988 by Ann Louise Gittleman. Reprinted by permission of Bantam Books.

"Basil Pesto." Reprinted by permission of Holly Jo Sollars.

"Bean Burritos." Reprinted by permission of Holly Jo Sollars.

"Caraway Butter." Reprinted by permission of Melissa Diane Smith.

"Cauliflower in Red Pepper Sauce" from *The Yeast Connection Cookbook*, by William Crook and Marjorie Hurt Jones. Copyright © 1989 by William Crook and Marjorie Hurt Jones. Reprinted by permission of Professional Books.

"Cheeseless Turkey Sausage Pizza." Reprinted by permission of Melissa Diane Smith.

"Chestnuts Roasted on an Open Fire" from *Deliciously Low*, by Harriet Roth. Copyright © 1983 by Harriet Roth. Used by permission of Dutton Signet, a division of Penguin Books USA Inc.

"Chicken Bouillon, Speedy Soup Mix & Onion Mustard" from *Deliciously Simple,* by Harriet Roth. Copyright © 1986 by Harriet Roth. Used by permission of Dutton Signet, a division of Penguin Books USA Inc.

"Chicken or Turkey Stock" from *Get the Sugar Out,* by Ann Louise Gittleman, M.S. Copyright© 1996 by Ann Louise Gittleman. Reprinted by permission of Harmony Books, a division of Crown Publishers, Inc.

"Fresh Herbal Tabouli." Reprinted by permission of Melissa Diane Smith.

"Garlic Broth." Reprinted by permission of Holly Jo Sollars.

"Greek-Style Spinach and Brown Rice." Reprinted by permission of Melissa Diane Smith.

"Greek Tszitziki Sauce" from *Get the Sugar Out,* by Ann Louise Gittleman, M.S. Copyright © 1996 by Ann Louise Gittleman. Reprinted by permission of Harmony Books, a division of Crown Publishers, Inc.

"Herb Dressing" from *The Healing Power* of Food, by Michael T. Murray, N.D. Copyright © 1993 by Michael T. Murray, N.D. Reprinted by permission of Prima Publishing, Rocklin, CA.

"Herbed Hamburgers" from *Cooking Without a Grain of Salt,* by Elma W. Bagg. Copyright © 1972 by Elma W. Bagg. Reprinted by permission of Doubleday Books.

"Jicama Chip Ole" from *Arizona Heart Institute Foundation Cookbook,* by the Arizona Heart Institute Foundation. Copyright © 1993 by the Arizona Heart Institute Foundation. Reprinted by permission of the Arizona Heart Institute Foundation.

"Lemony Almond Macaroon Drops" from *Get the Sugar Out,* by Ann Louise Gittleman, M.S. Copyright © 1996 by Ann Louise Gittleman. Reprinted by permission of Harmony Books, a division of Crown Publishers, Inc.

"Low Sodium Sausage" from *Secrets of Salt-Free Cooking,* by Jeanne Jones. Copyright © 1991 by Jeanne Jones. Reprinted by permission of Cole Publishing Group.

"Mediterranean Spinach Dip for Craites" from *Cooking for Healthy*

"Refried Beans." Reprinted by permission of Holly Jo Sollars.

"Roast Corn on the Cob" from *Healing with Whole Foods*, by Paul Pitchford. Copyright © 1993 by Paul Pitchford. Reprinted by permission of North Atlantic Books, Berkeley, CA.

"Senmief" from *Cooking for Healthy Healing*, 2nd Ed., by Linda Rector Page, N.D., Ph.D. Copyright © 1995 by Linda Rector Page, N.D., Ph.D. Reprinted by permission of Healthy Healing Publications.

"Sesame Lemon Dressing" from *Beyond Pritikin*, by Ann Louise Gittleman, M.S. Copyright © 1988 by Ann Louise Gittleman, M.S. Reprinted by permission of Bantam Books.

"Simple South of the Border Salsa" from *Super Nutrition for Women*, by Ann Louise Gittleman, M.S. Copyright © 1991 by Ann Louise Gittleman. Reprinted by permission of Bantam Books.

"Spiced Beef with Wine, Cuinga, and Garlic" from *Super Nutrition for Women*, by Ann Louise Gittleman, M.S. Copyright © 1991 by Ann Louise Gittleman. Reprinted by permission of Bantam Books.

"Spice Bean Dip" from *Feed Your Soul*, by George Fowler and Jeff Lehr. Copyright © 1993 by George Fowler and Jeff Lehr. Reprinted by permission of Glen Wimmer.

"Spicy Thai Shrimp Soup" from *Kitchen Herbs*, by Sal Gilbertie. Copyright © 1988 by Sal Gilbertie. Reprinted by permission of Bantam Books.

"Spring Minestrone" from *Super Nutrition for Menopause*, by Ann Louise Gittleman, M.S. Copyright © 1993 by Ann Louise Gittleman, M.S. Reprinted by permission of Simon & Schuster.

"Tandoori Chicken" reprinted from the award-winning book *Indian Recipes for a Healthy Heart* by Mrs. Lakhani, with permission of Fahil Publishing Company, Box 7000-310, Palos Verdes, CA 90274.

"Tempe, Lettuce, Tomato (T.L.T.)." Reprinted by permission of Holly Jo Sollars.

"Thai Peanut Dip." Reprinted by permission of Melissa Diane Smith.

"Tomato Sauce I." Reprinted by permission of Melissa Diane Smith.

"Turkey Sausage Pizza." Reprinted by permission of Melissa Diane Smith.

"Unsalted Chicken or Turkey Gravy" from *Secrets of Salt-Free Cooking*, by Jeanne Jones. Copyright © 1991 by Jeanne Jones. Reprinted by permission of Cole Publishing Group.

"Vegetarian Chile" from *The American Heart Association Low-Salt Cookbook.* Copyright © 1990 by The American Heart Association. Reprinted by permission of Random House, Inc.

"Wheat Free Banana Muffins" from *Back to Health*, by Dennis Remington and Barbara W. Higa, R.D. Copyright © 1986 by Dennis Remington and Barbara W. Higa, R.D. Reprinted by permission of Vitality House International, Inc.

"Winter Bean Pate" from *Super Nutrition for Menopause*, by Ann Louise Gittleman, M.S. Copyright © 1993 by Ann Louise Gittleman, M.S. Reprinted by permission of Simon & Schuster.

"The World's Best Bloody Mary." Copyright © 1994/1996 by Lang Naturals. Reprinted by permission of David Lang.

"Yesterday's Vegetables Become Today's Salad" from *Deliciously Low*, by Harriet Roth. Copyright © 1983 by Harriet Roth. Used by permission of Dutton Signet, a division of Penguin Books USA Inc.

INDEX